Quality of Life

Other Books Written by H. Stanley Jones:

Planning Your Financial Future:
Personal Financial Planning That Helps You

Marketing Your Financial Planning Services:
A Guide For Professionals

Contributing Author to:

Star Spangled Speakers

Audio Cassette Programs:

Personal Financial Planning

Personal Cash Management
and
Personal Tax Planning

Quality of Life

Achieving Balance in an Unbalanced World

By
H. Stanley Jones

KAUAI PRESS

Copyright © 1994 by H. Stanley Jones

All rights reserved. No part of this book may be reproduced or transmitted in any form or by any means electronic or mechanical — including photocopying, recording, or by any information storage or retrieval system — without written permission from Kauai Press, except for the inclusion of quotations in a review.

Copyediting by Sharon Mills
Jacket Design by Carol Haralson
Layout & Production by Rika Dotson

This publication is designed to provide accurate and authoritative information in regard to the subject matter covered. It is sold with the understanding that the publisher is not engaged in rendering legal, accounting, or other professional service. If legal advice or other expert assistance is required, the services of a competent professional person should be sought. *From a Declaration of Principles jointly adapted by a Committee of the American Bar Association and a Committee of Publishers.*

Library of Congress Cataloging-in-Publication Data

Jones. H. Stanley.
   Quality of life : achieving balance in an unbalanced
world / H. Stanley Jones.
   p. cm.
   Includes Index.
   Preassigned LCCN : 94-096087.
   ISBN 1-885161-07-8

   1. Quality of life -- United States.   I. Title.
HN160.J65 1994   306'.0973
                                   QBI94-833

Printed in the United States of America

Table of Contents

Acknowledgements & Dedication — vii

Foreword by Joe Batten, CPAE — 1

Preface by Arnold Fox, M.D. — 3

Introduction — 7

Chapter

   1 Family — Where It All Begins — 25

   2 Community — Staying Connected in an Unconnected World — 39

   3 Education — A Never-Ending Quest — 57

   4 Career — Love What You Do; Do What You Love — 73

   5 Finances — To Achieve Financial Independence, Start Early — 91

   6 Health — More Than Just Minding Body & Soul — 115

   7 Leisure — Avoid the Syndrome of All Work & No Play — 135

   8 Spirituality — Getting In Touch With Your Greater Self — 151

Conclusion — 167

Epilogue — 171

About the Author — 173

Index — 175

Quality of Life: Acknowledgments and Dedication

Acknowledgments and Dedication

Many people have materially contributed to the development and production of this book. The concept of Quality of Life has been brewing within me for a long time. I had been developing the ideas and plans for many years while collecting materials, notes, quotes, etc. The desire to write for quite a while had been just that — a desire. A desire is just a variation of "wishful thinking." What was lacking was a commitment — a plan of action — a decision to implement.

My "Someday Isle" — I'll write this book — was a dream just waiting to be born.

The number one person in my life has been *my number one supporter*, encourager and help mate. She is my *wonderful* wife, my life partner — she is Roberta Jones. Roberta has brought to me and to our marriage the most delightful and highest Quality of Life.

Therefore, with the deepest of gratitude, love and appreciation for all she has done and continues to do, enabling me to enjoy and appreciate the quality of our life together, I humbly dedicate this book to the most important person in my life, my wife, Roberta.

In addition, there are several other people whose assistance helped to make this book possible.

I want to acknowledge and thank our assistant, Rika Dotson, for her loyalty, devotion, dedication, and most of all, her consistent, upbeat, pleasant attitude. She has been a joy to work

with as well as having provided invaluable assistance in the production of the manuscript.

Little did I know when Sharon Mills, CPA started doing accounting work for me that she also possessed writing and editing skills. When we started to fine-tune the chapters, she volunteered comments and suggested ideas. Her significant efforts resulted in many improvements and expansion to the material. My deepest thanks and appreciation is hereby extended to Sharon.

Next, let me also express my appreciation to Sol Marshall who provided valuable editorial assistance. He rearranged many of my words, rejected some and substituted others deemed more appropriate, slightly changed a thought or an idea so as to give greater meaning. For his effort I say, "I wish your second eighty years of life will exceed the quality of your first eighty."

Leatrice Eiseman, renowned color specialist and Director of the Pantone Color Institute, identified colors which symbolically correlate as follows:

Subject	**Color**
Family	Earth tones
Community	Brick red
Education	Yellow
Career	Green
Finances	Blue
Health	Rose
Leisure	Orange
Spirituality	Purple

Quality of Life: Acknowledgments and Dedication

Numerous members of the National Speakers Association responded to questionnaires and interviews. To attempt to list the many contributors from this wonderful, loving, caring and sharing organization would take more space than the contents of the book. Let me just say I love you all and deeply appreciate your thoughtful comments and willingness to give of yourselves.

The following individuals each read and commented on all or a significant portion of the text. Many of their suggestions have been adopted and incorporated within the chapters.

If you like the results, they are to be complimented. If you don't, I accept full responsibility.

Dale Anderson, M.D.; Stephen Ash, Ph.D.; Joe Batten, CPAE; California State Senator Marian Bergeson; Jean-Louis Brindamour; Jack Canfield, CSP; Jean Crawford; Michael Crisp; Arnold Fox, M.D.; Mike Frank, CSP, CPAE; Robert Henry, CSP, CPAE; Bert Hughes; John B. Kelly, CFP; Art Linkletter, CPAE; Og Mandino, CPAE; Bishop James K. Mathews; Terry Paulson, Ph.D., CSP, CPAE; Jean C. Peterson; The Rev. Dr. William M. Pickard, Jr.; Dan Poynter; Nido Qubein, CSP, CPAE; Naomi Rhode, CSP, CPAE; Glenna Salsbury, CSP, CPAE; Mark Sanborn; Dave Tansey, Ed.D.; Carolyn Warner.

Grateful acknowledgment is made to the publishers and authors named below for permission to reprint the following material:

Poem *A Twisted Tale* used by permission of the author, Renee Spiering.

Excerpt from *Super Joy* by Paul Pearsall, M.D. Copyright ©1988 by Paul Pearsall. Used by permission of Doubleday, a division of Bantam Doubleday Dell Publishing Group, Inc.

Excerpt from *Using the Myers-Briggs Type Indicator in Organizations, 2nd Edition* by Sandra Krebs Hirsh, modified and reproduced by special permission of the Publisher, Consulting Psychologists Press, Inc., Palo Alto, CA 94303. Copyright © 1991 by Consulting Psychologists Press, Inc. [All rights reserved. Further reproduction is prohibited without the Publisher's written permission.]

Excerpt from *Further Along the Road Less Traveled*, COPYRIGHT © 1993 by M. Scott Peck, M.D. Reprinted by permission of Simon & Schuster, Inc.

Excerpt from *The Different Drum: Community Making and Peace* COPYRIGHT © 1987 by M. Scott Peck, M.D., P.C. Reprinted by permission of Simon & Schuster, Inc.

Excerpts from *The Bakersfield Californian* used by permission of *The Bakersfield Californian*.

> Page 51, Neighborhood Watch story "Rexland Acres Residents Battle Image Perpetuated by Recent Column" by Herb Benham.
>
> Page 159, Francis Hernandez story "AIDS - Infected Woman Takes Message to Kern Schools" by Tamara Welch.
>
> Page 160, Chuck Wall story "Students' Random Kindness Captures Public's Imagination" by Rick Bentley.
>
> Page 160, Sharon Brothers story "Respect - Junior High Students Get Lessons in Poise" by Connie Keeler.

Foreword
by
Joe Batten, CPAE

Here is a book that truly supplies balance. In a world that is literally aching for answers — for a way to go — H. Stanley Jones provides us with a smorgasbord of principles, values, guidelines and vision.

It is at once stimulating, challenging, insightful and reassuring. The tested verities *work*!

The reader will feel the wisdom, love, and commitment of Dr. Jones on every page. Mind, body, and spirit are all nurtured with the addition of practical hands-on road maps and checkpoints.

As a consultant to organizations who seek to build a *total quality culture*, it is my earnest hope that all of the people in such organizations will read and commit to *living* the contents of this book.

Unless you're ready for a richer, fuller, more balanced life, beware. After you've read this book thoughtfully again and again, you may never be the same.

Will you do it?

Joe Batten, CPAE, coined the phrase he lives by, "Be All That You Can Be." Joe is Chairman and CEO of The Batten Group, an international consortium of consultants, speakers, trainers and training products.

Besides being a speaker of great renown, he has produced training films, videos, and audio programs. Joe has also written several best-selling books including *Tough-Minded Management, Tough-Minded Leadership* and *Building A Total Quality Culture*.

Preface
by
Arnold Fox, MD

We have been told that the greatest discovery of the 20th Century was not the electric light nor the automobile, but the knowledge of the ability to change our lives by changing our attitudes and thoughts.

Tremendous changes have occurred in all facets of our daily lives — changes over which we feel we have no control. We have perceived many of these changes as having negative effects. We've lost faith in our ability to bring about positive change.

We see gigantic corporations, which in the past had only known expansion, now facing downsizing, plant closings and lay-offs of tens of thousands. Entire industries no longer exist.

Patients come to my office with symptoms of disease and the genesis of much of this disease lies in daily, stressful, unstable

living. People feel the ground slipping away. The old ways are rapidly leaving them and they feel exposed and not ready for the changes which are occurring. People are loosing their sense of security.

But many years ago MacArthur told us, "There is no security in this world; there is only opportunity."

Despite the battles going on in this world — actual warfare, economic and social changes, there is still great opportunity. Make no mistake about that!

Thank goodness, H. Stanley Jones has, at this time of great need, written this excellent book, *Quality of Life: Achieving Balance in an Unbalanced World.*

The book builds the foundation for the successful life — for the good, happy, contributing life — based on Stan Jones' eight factors or as he calls them, the eight spokes of a wheel. When all spokes are the same length, the wheel is in balance — in harmony — and the ride — life — is smoother.

As a physician with 37 years experience in ministering and treating patients, I can tell you with great certainty that the proper balance of the positive elements in your life are necessary for a successful life. I believe that success is contingent upon the choices we make. When we choose correctly, success is mirrored in every aspect of our lives. Stan Jones helps you make the choices that will undeniably enhance your life.

I highly recommend this book. I suggest that you first read it in its entirety, then spend some time rating, on a scale of 1-10,

Quality of Life: Preface

how your life scores for each of the eight factors. Start with the factor with the lowest score, and follow Stan Jones' suggestions for improving that factor. Do the same with the next lowest factor, and so on and so on.

As you follow the suggestions in the book, and make the appropriate choices to improve your life, update your scoring. You will continually correct your course and reach your destination — a successful life.

Family, Community, Education, Career, Finances, Health, Leisure and *Spirituality* — These are the signposts you are to use on the road to the goal of a successful life. You must always keep your signposts in sight, never lose track of them!

I urge you to enjoy the day — rejoice in the day — as you move toward your goal.

Get started immediately on this project for your personal success. Whatever you can do, or dream you can do — begin it.

Arnold Fox is a physician specializing in Internal Medicine with his practice in Beverly Hills. In addition, he is an Adjunct Professor at the University of the Pacific in the graduate course of Pain Studies. He is a former Assistant Professor of Medicine at the University of California, Irvine, California College of Medicine. He is also an Independent Medical Examiner (CME) for the State of California in Internal Medicine, Cardiology and Toxicology.

Dr. Fox (with his son, Barry Fox) has authored several books: *The Beverly Hills Medical Diet, DCPA to End Chronic Pain and Depression, Immune for Life, Wake Up! You're Alive, Making Miracles* and *Beyond Positive Thinking*, as well as hundreds of articles.

Introduction

What is life? What does it take to have a rich and fulfilling existence? Few of us have taken adequate time to plan fully for this enjoyable journey called life.

There is a story about a priest, a minister, and a rabbi discussing the age old question of when does life begin.

"The time of conception. At that time there is life." said the priest, rather obviously. "No," The minister replied, "not until there is a live birth. Up until then we don't really have a viable entity." The rabbi answered, "You are both wrong. I'll tell you when life begins. When the dog has died, and the kids have left home, that's when life begins!"

As entertaining as that story is, I am much less concerned about when life begins as I am about the extent to which life is experienced.

What gives "quality" to life? Why is it some people seem to have the Midas touch, living healthy, productive and loving lives, while others seem to fail at every endeavor?

Is it a matter of the genes we inherit or are we strictly a product of our environment? Is it early childhood influences or hard work as adults? Or is it a combination of all these factors and more?

Whatever the answer, I truly believe the quality of any life can be improved through studying and following the suggestions presented in this book. I want to assist you in becoming introspective, examining your inner-self and making decisions that will positively affect you and your future.

Remember the television series Fantasy Island? There are people who go through life dreaming about "Someday Isle." "Someday, I'll be rich and famous." "Someday, I'll find the cure for cancer." "Someday, I'll write a best-selling novel."

Almost everyone, at one time or another, has dreamed about winning the lottery, becoming a movie star, or some other far-fetched idea.

Certainly, there is no harm in occasional daydreams. But there is a real difference between daydreams of desires which assist in planning for the future and wild, fantastic, dreams.

A reporter interviewed a very well-to-do man approaching his eightieth birthday. The man was physically active and an avid

golfer. On his sixtieth birthday, he played three eighteen hole rounds from coast to coast — New York, Chicago and Los Angeles — in one day. On his seventieth birthday, he played three eighteen hole rounds in three different countries — Canada, United States and Mexico — in one day.

"What do you want to do on your eightieth birthday?" the reporter asked. "I want to play a round of golf on the moon." the man replied. "I'm ready, but science hasn't caught up to me yet. I guess I'll have to wait for my ninetieth birthday for that."

We know that living to be ninety or more is quite possible. We have to be careful in saying that civilian flight to the moon is an impossible dream.

> **The future belongs to those who believe in the beauty of their dreams.**
> **— Eleanor Roosevelt**

How do you separate fantasy dreams from attainable dreams?

Our Constitution requires that to be eligible to be President of the United States, one must be born a U.S. citizen. A non-native born person, then, is having a fantasy dream when he or she hopes and dreams of becoming President.

> My father had a lot of fantasy dreams. He once said he would give his right arm to play the piano. Even though one-armed piano players do exist, taking piano lessons and practicing would fulfill his dream far better than cutting off his right arm.

Attainable dreams are very effective when used for setting goals. The more definitive and specific you can be with your goals — if you can literally reach out and touch them, see them, smell them, taste them and practically hear them — the more likely they are to become reality.

Successful People

Successful people are dreamers who have found a dream too exciting, too important to remain in the realm of fantasy; who day by day, hour by hour, toil in the quest of those dreams until, one day, they can touch them with their hands and see them with their eyes.

Those desiring to be in the entertainment business need to take lessons, study with experts and perform at every opportunity. They may need to move to New York or Hollywood to be available for auditions. They will need to learn the business of show business and make valuable connections.

Aspiring writers must practice writing and have their writing critiqued. Writings cannot be just thoughts, they must be put to paper. Through practice, writers learn the little nuances of communication by using carefully chosen words.

Those who desire to advance a business career must take the appropriate courses, network with business executives, read business publications and learn to speak the language of business.

Quality of Life: Introduction

What are *you* doing, day by day, hour by hour, in the quest of your dreams so that one day you can touch them with *your* hands and see them with *your* eyes?

Are you spending leisure time studying subjects which will lead to the fulfillment of your goals or are you watching television, dreaming of your "Someday Isle"?

I want you to write down your hopes and dreams for the future. Be as specific as you can. Don't say you want a new car, or a better job, or to lose weight.

Instead, say "I want a new, four door, dark blue Ferrari with light blue leather interior, cellular phone and CD player."

Or, "I want to be Vice-President of my company within two years and earn a salary of $150,000."

Or, "Within six months, I want to weigh less than 130 pounds."

Give specifics which are realistic for *you* and which are truly *your* dreams for the near future. Put this book down now, take out pen and paper and write down *your* dreams.

> **Your vision will become clearer only when you can look into your own heart. Who looks outside, dreams. Who looks inside, awakens.**
> **— Carl Jung**

It helps to post a copy of your goals on your mirror or refrigerator so that you are continually reminded of what you are working toward. Give copies to your immediate family and closest friends. Seek their help and support in achieving your personal plans for the future. By sharing your aspirations, you are more likely to succeed.

> **Life is a paradise for those who love many things with a passion!**
> **— Leo Buscaglia**

Goals tackled with deep commitment and passion are more likely to be achieved than tasks undertaken with a lackadaisical, ho-hum approach and attitude.

While coaching a hesitant speaker, Dr. Kenneth McFarland challenged him by saying, "If your daughter were on the gallows, accused of a crime you know she did not commit, and the odds of her living were up to you and your ability to deliver an impassioned plea to the potential executors, don't you think you could speak with real passion to save her life?"

"Of course I could." the man replied.

Isn't that true for all of us? If something is truly life-threatening, we are able to rise above the norm to perform. Think how much more we could accomplish if we tackled every assignment with this same passion.

> **Life is either a daring adventure, or nothing.**
> **— Helen Keller**

Quality of Life: Introduction

The opportunity is yours to make a daring adventure out of life — maybe not every moment of every day, but many good, positive moments can lead to a lifetime of wonderful enjoyment.

Intentional living leaves each of us with the challenge of making each day significant. Life is too valuable to risk boring ourselves.
— Terry Paulson, Ph.D., CSP, CPAE

Just as you come to a fork in the road and have to decide between right or left, likewise, you have decisions in life. Do or not do; go or not go; invest your time, effort, resources and talents in this direction or that direction; spend time with friends or strangers; watch sitcoms or read about subjects of importance.

To change one's life: start immediately — do it flamboyantly — no exceptions.
— William James

It's not easy, but you can change your life for the better. Some people are reluctant to start journeys or explore opportunities, for fear they might not succeed.

What would you attempt if you knew you could not fail?
— Dr. Robert Schuller

You would approach every new adventure with the optimism of success. While everything you try in life will not turn out as you expect, you will not have failed if you have made an honest attempt. Each disappointment can be tempered with the knowledge you learned in the effort. Remember, you've automatically failed if you don't even try.

> **A wise man will make more opportunities than he finds.**
> — **Sir Francis Bacon**

Don't routinely close the door on opportunity. Be open and receptive to the unknown. There is little to be gained by failing to make an attempt.

In searching for a definition of "Quality of Life," I asked numerous people what "Quality of Life" meant to them.

First, let me share with you some excerpts from Art Linkletter's response. He states ". . .I am very curious personally, interested in trying to be better, do better, and know more."

Linkletter goes on to say, "I persist in accepting challenges that follow Milton's precept that a 'man's reach should exceed his grasp,' and finally I am constantly striving to prioritize my life so that I am doing things I truly enjoy, with people I truly care about. My motto is — things turn out best for the people who make the best of the way things turn out."

Before reading the other responses, write down your personal definition of "Quality of Life."

Quality of Life: Introduction

To have a balanced life — enjoying good health, sharing with good friends, carrying out a solid purpose of service and otherwise being physically fit, mentally active and spiritually balanced.
— **Nido Qubein, CSP, CPAE**

Spending as much time as possible together with my spouse. Determining my success based upon the number of nights I spend with my wife with our heads on the same pillow. Spending as much time with my kids as possible. Being able to attend as many of kids' personal functions as possible. Taking my wife with me on as many business trips as possible.
— Mike Frank, CSP, CPAE

A good life is when you can laugh more than you cry, you surround yourself with positive and loving people, and when you can go to bed and put your head on the pillow . . . you sleep soundly.
— **Ruth L. Klein**

To live so that when I meet my maker, he will not ask me why I was not more like this person or that person, but that he will tell me he is proud of me for filling the blueprint he visualized when he created me.
— Dottie M. Walters, CSP

Riding my motorcycle. If I had more money I would buy more toys and obtain added coaching for my professional skills.
— Jim Cathcart, CSP, CPAE

Living life to the fullest. I know how to do this through meaningful livelihood and relationships and a healthy mind and body.
— Marilyn Manning, Ph.D., CSP

To always have purpose in life, in relationships, and in work. To fulfill my ambitions as well as my potential. To be an ethical, moral person who is highly successful but never forget from whence I came. To spend my time and talent helping others to achieve their ambitions and potential.
— Thomas W. Faranda

The bottom line is love.
— Susan Donnelly

To live life to overflowing, having time to learn, money to give whatever I want, and to be physically/mentally strong.
— Eileen McDargh, CSP

Leave the world a better place than it was when I arrived — and have a lot of fun doing it.
— James W. Newman, CPAE

To feel fulfilled — and to help others.
— Elizabeth Jeffries, CSP

Quality of Life: Introduction

Abide by the Golden Rule while making a positive difference.

— **Burt Dubin**

Becoming a fully developed, fully functioning, self-actualizing person.
— Mark Victor Hansen, CSP

Quality of Life for me means looking forward to each day the moment I get up finding some value I can give and receive each day. It also means being spiritually sound and strong in faith and being physically healthy and vibrant.
— **Lou Heckler, CSP, CPAE**

Finding joy in each day, retiring fulfilled.
— Virgil Beasley, Psy.D.

To own my peace of mind.
— **Sidney Madwed**

For me, a high Quality of Life can only be accomplished by spending my time with my "passion" areas of interest. Managing my time around the people and projects I care for are vital. Since we cannot do everything we might love to do, due to human life-span limitations, one must focus.
— Daniel Burrus, CSP, CPAE

Now that you have an idea of how some define a quality life, how do you go about achieving your own quality life?

I have found the way to achieve a quality life is through maintaining the following eight factors in harmony with each other.

A wheel with eight spokes requires each spoke to be of the same length to ensure a smooth ride. Likewise, each of these eight elements — *Family, Community, Education, Career, Finances, Health, Leisure, Spirituality* — needs to be in balance to minimize the ruts and detours as you travel along life's way.

As we briefly explore descriptions of each spoke, rate your satisfaction with each factor on a scale from 1 to 10.

Family

A priority for many people is *family*.

What a joy and a blessing it is to thoroughly enjoy most of your family members most of the time! When things are tough and you are down and out, you can usually count on at least one family member to support you.

While some friends become like family, other special relationships endure for a time and then one or the other of you moves on. However, your family will generally stick with you through thick and thin — good times and bad!

Should there be conflict in one of your family relationships, seriously consider reconciling and resolving the problem. Isn't it

sad to hear someone say at a funeral, "I wish I had taken the time to tell them I loved them," or "I appreciated the things they did for me, I just never got around to saying so," "Why didn't I spend more time with them?"

COMMUNITY

Community is explored in a broader context than just the city where you live. Community may include your neighborhood, various social, fraternal, or religious groups or political boundaries. It means giving back to your community and not always taking from it.

Be an active participant working *for* something or somebody, rather than just *opposing* people and issues. And yes, this could include political involvement as well. Find issues and candidates whose views coincide with your own and then *work* for them.

Learn to value others *for*, not *in spite of*, their differences. We all have contributions to make.

EDUCATION

Education encompasses all learning experiences and is more than just formal classroom activities. The pursuit of education should be a continual, life-long process enjoyed for itself, not only as a necessary requirement for a specific goal.

Participate in seminars and workshops; explore new avenues through reading, listening, watching, attending, and participating. Be like a sponge, always absorbing and seeking

more knowledge. Constantly improve and refine your personal database.

Don't let your educational endeavors end when you receive your diploma or degree. Let those accomplishments be the beginning.

Where do ideas come from? Everywhere! Always be alert to new thoughts. Keep asking yourself, "What can I learn from this situation?"

CAREER

A major objective in achieving a high quality of life is to have a rewarding and productive *career*.

Most of us spend many of our waking hours at work. Really enjoying this primary activity is vital to having a sense of accomplishment and a feeling of acceptance. If you dread going to work, it is difficult to face the day with enthusiasm and vigor.

Which do you generally look forward to the most — Monday or Friday?

If your answer is most often "Friday," is it because the weekend represents a reprieve from the daily drudgery of 9 to 5? If so, maybe you should consider a career change.

Every Monday morning is not going to be a tremendous joy. However, Monday will provide pleasurable thoughts more times than not, if you truly enjoy your chosen career.

Quality of Life: Introduction

FINANCES

Finances is not about possessing a tremendous net worth or sizable current income, but rather providing an adequate income for today, tomorrow and the years to come. You want the ability to enjoy life and realize your basic needs and desires, to meet bills when due and to be able to retire with confidence.

A great number of people reach retirement age without the financial capacity to stop working. Many are required to rely upon relatives or welfare or must continue to be gainfully employed to survive.

Frivolous and reckless spending usually has its price. It may be just an economic cost, or it can lead to emotional problems, family difficulties and, occasionally, even suicide.

Keep your financial house in order, know what you have, what you need, and plan for your future by regularly saving along the way for those rainy days.

HEALTH

Optimum *health* positively affects all the areas of your life and makes every endeavor possible. Health refers to both your physical and mental well-being.

We have only one body. While some of the parts may be replaced or repaired, the basic structure needs to be cared for on a regular basis lest it wear out before you are ready to give it up.

Eating nutritious food, exercising regularly, observing sensible safety rules, learning to manage the stress in your life, getting adequate rest, and seeking help for emotional stress all contribute to healthy minds and bodies.

A meaningful quality of life cannot be achieved without robust health.

LEISURE

Leisure time is a reprieve from the normal routine. You will want to find pastimes which are fulfilling, stimulating, pleasurable and relaxing.

Some activities are enjoyed with friends and family, while others are engaged in alone. Whether an activity is leisure or work depends largely on your perception.

Effective time management is essential to ensure adequate opportunities for leisure endeavors. You will learn to delegate and stop procrastinating.

Leisure activities are easily combined with other quality of life factors to provide a balanced life.

SPIRITUALITY

Spirituality has to do with your personal beliefs and ethical practices. It is your relationship with the vital principles influencing life. Spirituality need not be the same as religion. Some religious people may not really be spiritual and some spiritual people may not feel religious.

Quality of Life: Introduction

Differing forms of the Golden Rule provide a positive guideline for ethical behavior. There are many ways to help others, but offering a helping hand instead of a hand-out produces longer lasting results.

Learning to forgive is essential to spiritual health. Hate destroys the one who hates, not the who is hated.

How did you score on each of the eight factors? If your satisfaction level is a 10 for one factor, but only a 3 or 4 for others, your life is out of balance. No matter how commendable that one factor may be, as your wheel goes down the road, it is going to produce a rough journey.

Start making changes in the areas of your life where you are experiencing the most dissatisfaction. Getting started isn't always easy, but the second step will be easier than the first. I promise the results will be rewarding.

My dream is for you to achieve success and happiness by keeping your life in balance while traveling the road of life. You can make the changes — it just takes commitment and decisions with passion.

> **Don't be afraid to take a big step if one is indicated. You can't jump a chasm in two small jumps.**
> **— David Lloyd George**

24

Chapter 1

Family — Where It All Begins

For years the traditional family was most accurately reflected in the television series, *Father Knows Best*, as a father, mother and three children.

That concept of family has changed significantly over the past 20 to 30 years. There are more divorces and remarriages; more unwed mothers and fathers; more grandparents raising their grandchildren; more people foregoing parenthood and more couples living together outside of marriage.

Today's family is often comprised of members unrelated through blood or marriage — step-parents, step-siblings, half-siblings and others for which there are no familial terms. Just because the members of a household are not related, does it necessarily make those members any less a family?

Family, in another context, is our biological relatives whether through birth or adoption — grandparents, parents, children, grandchildren, brothers, sisters, aunts, uncles and cousins — but family can mean much more.

Generally, in this wider definition, we limit "family" to relatives we know and with whom we maintain contact.

Finally, very close, intimate friends are often considered as family.

> **The family is the nucleus of civilization.**
> **— Will and Ariel Durant**

Invariably we find our most meaningful relationships are those we have with our families.

Healthy families have several traits in common. The first and most important is the ability to truly love and respect one another.

> **A friend loves you for your intelligence, a mistress for your charm, but your family's love is unreasoning; you were born into it and are of its flesh and blood. Nevertheless it can irritate you more than any group of people in the world.**
> **— Andre Maurois**

Is there anything quite as wonderful or frustrating as family?

Quality of Life: Family

"I'm the baby, gotta love me," was the catch phrase from a recent television series, and isn't that how we sometimes feel about our families? Gotta love them — they're my family. But can you love them even during those times when you don't even like them?

> **If you can't get rid of the family skeleton,
> you may as well make it dance.**
> — George Bernard Shaw

While we cannot control or be responsible for the acts of our relatives, we should stand by them when doing so will not compromise our basic principles and values.

Everybody wants and needs to be loved. However, some acts may be so despicable that we wonder who in the world could ever love a person who has committed those acts.

Yet, close relatives so love the individual that while they may not accept or condone the "act," they still love the person.

A father once said while disciplining his child, "I love you very much. However, I do not approve of your actions. I am punishing you for your wrongful actions, but I want you to know I still love *you*." Thereby, the father explained the separation between his disapproval of the actions from disapproval of the individual.

We often take our family for granted. After an especially stressful day on the job, some people come home and vent their frustrations on their family. People who wouldn't dream of yelling

at their boss or co-workers think nothing of yelling at the people who love them most.

If you find yourself acting in this manner, try to break the habit. Don't the people you love deserve the most consideration and respect?

Your children need your presence more than your presents.
— **Jesse Jackson**

A family spends quality time together, whether it's helping with homework, taking trips to the beach, sharing a hug, or just talking quietly. These activities build the bonds and memories that sustain us throughout our lifetime.

In a cartoon, a father states, "I try to spend time with my teenage daughter but her idea of *quality time* is a new Swatch watch."

Professional speaker, Lou Heckler told me how he learned about the importance of family.

"When our son was small, he was a very ill person . . . even near death at one dramatic point. We learned very early what is and isn't important in life. We operate in a simple fashion and keep our relationship open and honest. We focus on acquiring good times together, not material objects. When you suffer as you

Quality of Life: Family

watch your baby suffer, getting well and staying well in order to enjoy good times together seems like all there is. It still seems that way to us."

> Family members need to be able to give and receive comfort, appreciation and acceptance as needed. They are with you through good times and bad, and do the things for you that you would do for yourself if you were able.

Todd was a teenager who got in trouble with the police while his parents were out of town. His Aunt Karen learned of his incarceration and immediately bailed him out.

Karen didn't call Todd's father and say, "Hey, look what I've just done for you...", "How nice I am..." and so forth. Her reaction was "Of course I helped Todd out. You would have done the same for me, had it been my son. It's no big deal."

She then went on to comment, "When my son suffered a drug overdose, you were at the hospital with us. There was no discussion about what a terrible thing Matt had done. You offered consolation, compassion and support at the time of our need."

> **Where does the family start? It starts with a young man falling in love with a girl — no superior alternative has yet been found.**
> **— Sir Winston Churchill**

Another aspect of a healthy family is a solid marriage or loving relationship.

I know there are single parents out there raising functioning families, but these single parents have a much harder time.

Children with single-parents or step-families are more likely to have developmental, learning and emotional problems than children from intact families. It naturally follows that these troubled children are also more likely to become juvenile delinquents.

It is unfortunate to note that nearly half of all children in the United States can expect to live part of their childhood with a single parent.

> **A good marriage is like an incredible retirement fund. You pay everything you have into it during your productive life, and over the years it turns from silver to gold to platinum.**
> **— Willard Scott**

The makings of a good marriage or loving relationship are much the same as for a healthy family: love and respect, time alone together (without the kids), and the giving and taking of comfort, appreciation and acceptance.

A good marriage should have the foundation of a good friendship coupled with a fulfilling sexual relationship.

The difference between a spouse and other family members is the degree of intimacy — the deep sharing of one another on both a physical and emotional level.

Quality of Life: Family

"*LOVERS, PARTNERS, FRIENDS.* These are the passwords for a good marriage," said Steve as he smiled at his wife. "Janine is my very best friend. I trust her with my most intimate secrets and we have fun together. She always laughs at my jokes — even the ones she's heard twenty times. At the same time, she is my life partner. We work together to do the best for our children and to build our future. And best of all, she's a warm, generous lover."

"Of course, occasionally we fight," added Janine, "sometimes long and loud. But underneath, always is trust and our commitment to each other."

In even the closest families, relationships are not always harmonious — disagreements will occur. Sometimes those disagreements are extremely serious, perhaps seemingly irreconcilable.

Most families can be dysfunctional from time to time and to varying degrees. That's because families are made up of people — imperfect people with problems, emotions and agendas of their own.

Being a dysfunctional family doesn't mean that the family members don't love each other, just that the family doesn't function as well as it should or could.

We read about families where physical and emotional abuse are a way of life. Unfortunately, abuse in the childhood years seems to breed succeeding generations of abusers. Low self-esteem contributes to the problem, making the abuser feel the need to bring others down and the victim feel deserving of the mistreatment.

These highly dysfunctional families suffer from a very real illness and cannot become healthy without some kind of outside intervention.

Often problems are caused or intensified by drugs or alcohol, in which case the user needs to be treated for the addiction. Afterwards, the problem may not be solved because the other family members may have been enablers and find their roles hard to abandon.

Enablers are those who allow an addict to remain an addict. Even though they may hate the addiction or other self-destructive behavior itself, they subtly reinforce the behavior by covering up for the addict's transgressions and through other means. Enablers may unconsciously do this to feel important, superior, helpful or to justify addictions of their own.

To be successful, therapy for addicts often needs to involve the whole family. A disease such as alcoholism, drug addiction or abuse of any kind impacts the entire family. Everyone must learn to cope with and ultimately resolve the problems in the relationship.

A Twisted Tale

Once upon a time a group of people lived together
Lonely, separate, scared

They lived together and yet alone
A family by definition
Anything but by reality

Torn apart by ghosts from the past
Living in parents of the present

Years passed, pain came and receded
Yet never went away

They, the children, grew and went away
Years passed, new families began, parents of their own

Now they fought the pain
Alone, inside
Until they reached out to each other

And found the strength that they lacked alone
To fight the pain
To release the past
And they grew

Together they learned
To live, to love, to grow.

— Renee Spiering

I urge you to resolve family conflicts, to reconcile and to be willing to forgive. Whether or not you can totally forget, you have the capacity to forgive.

If you cannot forgive and accept yourself, you may have difficulty forgiving and accepting your relatives.

Aaron has an interesting theory about making up. He believes that when the person who made the mistake will not apologize, the person who was right should take the first step. Say something to the effect of, "I guess that I didn't make myself clear" or "Did I do something wrong?" or "I must have done something to offend you. Why don't I see you around anymore?"

This will provide an opportunity for the other person to open up in a non-threatening and friendly atmosphere.

Disagreements need not last forever. Sometimes all it takes is a simple "I'm sorry," "Please accept my apology," "I was wrong," "I misunderstood," or "I am sorry for what I did or said."

It is important to use "I" , rather than "You" statements. Not "You did ...", but rather "I ..." It may be, "I become angry when you do this. It is not that you cause me to feel angry, rather my reaction to your actions is one of anger in me."

> Often only an apology stands between
> keeping a friend or making an enemy.

At times, we unofficially adopt friends as family. This tends to occur when, as the result of distance, death or even estrangement, blood relatives are not available to take their rightful

Quality of Life: Family

place in the family. In these cases, close friends may be substituted for family, and in doing so, actually become part of the family.

> **Friends are family we choose for ourselves.**
> **— Sharon Mills**

There are all types of friends. Some friends are little more than acquaintances — people with whom we may have lunch or shop. Other friends are those with whom we work, but have no contact with away from the job. There are friends with whom we play basketball or enjoy watching sports. We also have neighborhood friends with whom we share a cup of coffee and gardening tips.

But the friend who becomes family is the friend you treasure — the one you open up to and with whom you share your inner most thoughts.

> **The Bond That Links Your True Family**
> **Is Not One Of Blood,**
> **But Of Respect And Joy In Each Other's Life.**
>
> **Rarely Do Members Of One Family**
> **Grow Up Under The Same Roof.**
>
> **— Richard Bach**

Carol and Susan are two women sharing a lifelong friendship. These two ladies, now in their mid-fifties, have been friends since second grade. They treat each other as sisters and their families think of them as sisters. In fact, it was not until Susan's children were adults that they realized Carol was not their biological aunt, but a close friend of their mother.

They've supported each other through marriage, divorce, births and deaths. "No matter what the circumstances, I always know I can count on Carol and she knows I'll always be there for her," states Susan.

Of course, women don't have the market cornered on close friendships.

Fred and Russell met when they were teenagers. Over the past 50 years they have remained friends despite attending different colleges, being in different branches of the armed services, choosing different livelihoods, and living in different cities. They have experienced marriage, children, health problems, retirement, family crises and disagreements. They are still friends who share each others lives, spend holidays together and look out for one another. Each thinks of the other as a family member.

The Carters are a childless couple who, through their church activities, adopted a foreign student.

They provided financial support to Kim and corresponded with him for many years. Through the Carters' support, Kim came to the United States, attended a seminary and became a minister.

Even though Kim and the Carters were worlds apart geographically and culturally, they referred to each other as "parents" and "child" and frequently visited each other following Kim's arrival in the United States.

Their relationship was just as solid and significant to the two adoptive parents as to the young man and the Carters could not have loved Kim more if he had actually been born into their family.

These examples demonstrate acceptance into a family based on true friendship. There is often a greater love and appreciation between friends than what might be between blood relations.

Occasionally friends from childhood become like family and remain friends to the end, while other friends come and go throughout our lives.

As you reflect back on you childhood days, do you remember your neighbors? How about the schoolmates you would never be apart from? You may even have made a vow, signing it in blood, that you were never going to be parted. Do you know where they are now? What they are doing? The odds are good that either they or you moved away and you have lost contact with each other. That is the way of life. True friendship involves special qualities that can't be manufactured or rushed.

We should enjoy and appreciate our friends while we have them. Let them enter into our world of friendship, but be willing to let them go when, and if, the time comes.

The joys and comforts of a warm and close-knit family — no matter how that family is defined — cannot be overrated.

Family members love one another without regard to blemishes, weight, baldness, beauty, or financial position. Families simply love. They accept and they forgive.

When there is true family spirit, love prevails and disagreements can be overlooked or worked out. It is important for us to accept and love one another. All love is not the same. Family love is different from spiritual love, friendship love and romantic love. The intensity and feeling of love may vary, but should always be there.

Chapter 2

Community — Staying Connected In An Unconnected World

What do you mean when you think of community? What is your community?

Some might be tempted to identify their community as the area where they live. Communities grow up around high schools and colleges, factories, dams, valleys and mountain tops. They may even develop out of an attempt to establish a separate identity from a major metropolis — such as Nob Hill or Brooklyn.

> But a community can be much more than a geographic location — it is a network, a sharing of kindred spirits. A community can be any collection of individuals who share a common interest or bond. We each belong to communities which change as our focus, interests, geographical location and other situations change.

Your communities can encompass every facet of your life, be it social, professional, spiritual, or political. You can belong to communities focused on common interests in religious convictions, recreational pursuits, political causes, special interests, or cultural and artistic interests.

You may even develop a community of people with whom you are in touch (many whom you have not and may never meet in person) through the use of computer bulletin boards, shareware, radio hams, pen pal organizations, or telephone party lines. It's been found some people are more able to "open up" through these anonymous connections.

The PRODIGY® Interactive Personal Service and CompuServe are two of the growing number of computer bulletin boards with over two million members between them. The PRODIGY Service notes "many members tell us that they value the sense of *community* they've developed through communicating with other like-minded individuals on our boards."

One of my employees collects shot glasses. Sue placed a notice on a computer bulletin board for collectors inquiring if there were others who shared her hobby. Several people responded with everything from information on books about shot glasses and their value to offers of exchanging glasses. While on the board, she also discovered many were surprised to learn there were other "serious" shot glass

collectors. Several said they had never "met" or heard of another collector until the subject appeared on the bulletin board. What a wonderful way to expand your horizons (and Sue's collection)!

The current popularity of radio and television call-in shows such as Rush Limbaugh, Larry King, Phil Donahue, Oprah Winfrey and Sally Jessy Raphäel point to the need people have to interact with others, even if only through telephone lines and radio waves. There is also the connection between those who watch the same programs and enjoy sharing the experience.

What is being suggested here is having very broad-based communities.

When you hear "community," you may think of your own neighborhood, city, county, state, nation and then even the world. The further you get from home, the larger your communities tend to become. When you meet a person in your hometown, you might say, "Oh, you live on the South side, so do I" thereby establishing a sense of community by living in the same neighborhood. If you're traveling abroad and meet a fellow American, you realize that your sense of community has expanded to encompass the entire country.

People are lonely because they build walls instead of bridges.
— Joseph F. Newton

I spoke to a woman one time who went to a church in South East Asia and she exclaimed, "They were singing the same songs I sing in my church in California." This expanded her concept of community, providing a feeling of togetherness in mutual interest and involvement in the same form of religious worship.

> Think about your own neighborhood. Do you make newcomers feel welcome? Do you acquaint them with the life of the locality, your favorite shops, traffic patterns to be aware of, along with other helpful tips? Or are you like the vast majority of disconnected Americans who aren't even aware new people have moved in or old ones have left?

The lack of a community seems to be the norm in larger cities. In smaller, more Midwest cities, people do not move as often and the community roots are much deeper and the bonding is much tighter.

> Small communities create a sense of personal power. When people are connected, *anyone's* pain is *everyone's* pain. If Farmer Smith's barn burns down, the community works together to build him a new one.

The peaks and valleys of living are shared by all in a small community — a death is mourned by all; the joy of a wedding or birth celebrated by all.

> People living in larger communities have become observers, watching death and destruction on the six o'clock news and realizing the problems are too big to be solved alone. Since they are not connected, they tend to feel powerless instead of empowered.

Quality of Life: Community

Periodically, we hear stories about passersby ignoring someone in dire need, crossing the street rather than getting involved, leaving that person to fend alone.

Quality communities operate in an atmosphere of love, peace and harmony, of pulling together for the good of all and not at the expense of any single person.

An integral part of any quality community is the importance of fostering individualism and differences while continuing to maintain a sense of togetherness and commonality.

Quality communities allow for and accept differences. We often grow more through encounters with those who have different beliefs and philosophies because they stimulate and challenge us.

There was a California assemblyman by the name of B.T. Collins. He was different in that:

- He lost an arm and a leg in Vietnam.

- He served as Chief of Staff to the Democratic governor Jerry Brown, while he was a committed Republican.

- During California's Medfly infestation, he drank Malathion to prove that the dosage to be sprayed over the infested area wasn't dangerous to human health.

- As head of the California Conservation Corps, he adopted the realistic motto, "Hard work, low pay, miserable conditions."

- He fired people for making racist, sexist or homophobic remarks — before these actions became politically correct.

- He framed his hate mail and hung it on the wall.

- He would speak up and speak out on many issues sometimes creating an enemy by his forthrightness, other times creating a friend who appreciated his willingness to stand up for his beliefs.

- In spite of (or because of) his differences, he was a person who did contribute.

There are certainly many others who dare to be different and gain respect in the community as a result.

Gifts Differing by Isabell Briggs Myers in conjunction with her son, Peter B. Myers, is a book extolling the concept that each of us has gifts; many of these gifts differ and the differences can create beauty, harmony and completeness.

Maya Angelou, in her book, *Wouldn't Take Nothing for My Journey Now*, puts it this way. "It is a time for parents to teach young people early on that in diversity there is beauty and there is strength. We all should know that diversity makes for a rich tapestry, and we must understand that all the threads of the tapestry are equal in value no matter their color; equal in importance no matter their context."

Quality of Life: Community

If you choose to disparage, rather than value differences, you will find a reason not to be a part of a community or not to associate with someone who is different from you.

Our differences are truly gifts and we should appreciate, be happy and rejoice in the gifts rather than letting them lead to estrangement.

Communities are multi-faceted and have characteristics which may vary under stress. Like seeds, communities grow, develop and expand. This multi-faceted quality is similar to that of a rough-hewn gemstone whose real qualities are brought out through much cutting and polishing, creating a high quality jewel, or in this case, a community. But this process takes time and commitment.

One problem is that some communities develop a form of exclusiveness — cliques. If you are not *a part* of the clique then you are *apart* from them or separated. It may be difficult to break in.

While communities may have cliques and factions which choose sides, quality communities have been able to work beyond that to find a common identity that is enriched by the differences. When that common identity breaks down, groups segregate, walls and boundaries are formed, the spies are chosen, blaming begins and community gives way to chaos and conflict. To have quality of life, we must have connections, not constant conflict.

The characteristic of a true community is not isolationism, but togetherness.

Successful communities search for ways to reach out — to extend themselves to be inclusive rather than exclusive. Members of a true community have a commitment, a willingness and a desire to co-exist by building stronger bonds. They are not trying to find ways to separate and exclude because of some difference.

My colleague, Hope Mihalap defines a quality life as, "one in which you can manage to pay your bills, laugh with people you love, and respect your surroundings. This last is always threatened, alas, by ever-present bigotry and pollution. A life of good quality would have less of these."

> Bigotry is pollution of the soul. Don't choose groups whose main reason for existence is to promote hate and bigotry. You can't be a friend to everyone, but you need not be an enemy, either.

Being an integral and quality member of a community requires a degree of commitment, similar to that found in a successful marriage. It requires that you don't give up when the going gets rough, as part of the roughness is what smooths future roads and builds strength of character.

If you experience hardships and difficulties together, you have strengthened your bond and can later experience greater difficulties with less trauma because you have endured successfully before. Each person is a vital part of a quality community.

> **No man is an island, entire of itself; every man is a piece of the continent, a part of the main ... any man's death diminishes me, because I am involved in mankind ...**
> **— John Donne**

When Roy was alive, he and Theresa belonged to a social group of couples. Following the death of her husband, Theresa wanted to continue in the group. "I was feeling very lonely without Roy, and really needed the support of my friends.

"However, they started excluding me from their activities. Finally, one of the women told me it was because they were afraid I would try to take one of their husbands. Of course, I wasn't the least bit interested in any of them. Not only did I lose my Roy, but I also lost my friends."

Find ways to give back to your community, support your concerns, and help support that which others have done. Be a giver in order to be a receiver. Don't be a perpetual sponge.

Well known speaker, Terry Paulson, Ph.D., CSP, CPAE, says, "Relationships are like deposit systems. If you don't put anything in, don't expect to get anything out. Try it with your bank. Ask the manager, 'This year would you mind if I just made withdrawals?' I think we all know the answer to that one. Put something into your community if you ever expect to get something back."

As a teenager, Nido Qubein immigrated from Lebanon with $50 in his pocket and very little command of the English language. Combining hard work, skill, and intelligence with a little luck resulted in an American success story. I asked Nido about his philosophy of life and this is what he told me: "I believe that life is a journey through which we have many opportunities to be useful and to serve others. To the extent that we can make a difference in other people's lives, we truly make a contribution to our world.

"I implement this philosophy in my daily life by dedicating one-third of my life to learning, one-third of my life to earning and one-third of my life to serving. I am involved extensively in my community, my church and serve on national boards. I don't mind stepping forward and giving of my time, effort and money to make good things happen.

"You don't help others so that others will help you in return. You do it because it's your obligation as a member of humanity. It makes you a contributor to the human cause, and not a taker. The biblical principle is also a universal principle: Those who give much also receive much. If you give from your heart, others will give from their hearts in return, and you become a sharer in human generosity. I have been blessed with a successful career, which has enabled me to do many things for my family, my community, my state and my country."

> **Don't give until it hurts. Give until it feels good.**
> **— Unknown**

Even though we may not have children in school, most of us are part of school district communities. Support is needed for the local high school band, scout activities, and children selling cookies, candies or tickets.

Quality of Life: Community

If you do have children in school, being an active, involved participant in the Parent Teacher Association is one way to be a quality member of the community.

Trade cynicism for activism — get involved!

— Terry Paulson

Within your city, take part in being *for* selected issues rather than just being *opposed*. Support candidates for office. Find causes in which you believe and are interested — then work for them. Being a part of a political victory can be very elating and satisfying.

While support of a losing cause can be disheartening, you will still have the satisfaction of knowing you tried — that you became involved. You have to put forth some effort. Good will does not automatically, magically happen.

The job of a citizen is to keep his mouth open.
— Günter Grass

Contribute even if you feel the position you support is a "lost cause." If you speak, you will be heard and your efforts can influence the ultimate outcome. You may not get everything you want, but you will put the winning side on notice that they are not without opposition.

The only thing necessary for the triumph of evil is for good men to do nothing.
— **Edmund Burke**

There are issues of concern in city and county governments. An example is the annexation of unincorporated territories. Investigate why you should support one side or the other. Then contribute your time and dollars. Lend your name in public support for the side on which you stand.

I believe that every right implies a responsibility; every opportunity, an obligation; every possession, a duty.
— **John D. Rockfeller, Jr.**

The same concept can be expanded into state issues. Again, find the side of importance to you, become involved, stand up, speak up and support issues to help your community grow and prosper. Thereby, you may also grow and prosper.

The word "prosper" here has far more meaning than just economic enhancement. There is the good feeling of knowing you have participated. That you did take a stand. That you are willing to be counted, to be seen, to be acknowledged as an "activist" versus a "passivist." In their song, *I Am A Rock*, musicians Paul Simon and Art Garfunkel state this premise well — "I'd rather be a hammer than a nail."

A homeowner's association is an excellent example of a group of people sharing the common interests of maintaining

Quality of Life: Community

beauty, keeping the grounds clean, or solving health, safety and security problems.

> **Good citizenship applies the power of the ballot ... The good citizen keeps his house painted, his lawn trimmed and flowers growing in his garden. He champions worthy causes and helps the unfortunate. He strives to be a good neighbor and to do well the thousand and one little things that add up to the big things we all want.**
> **— Unknown**

Community efforts can be seen in Neighborhood Watch committees, or ad hoc neighborhood committees formed to address specific problems such as vandalism or traffic control. Not only do these organizations create a higher quality of life by encouraging peace and harmony, they also increase the value of your property by creating a desirable neighborhood environment.

Recently, my local newspaper, *The Bakersfield Californian*, ran a story about two women who had formed a Neighborhood Watch group in an area of town plagued by drug dealers and addicts. "What we'd like to do is have a welcoming committee and take the newcomers a dish," Barbara McMurray said. "Then we'd like to tell them the way it's going to be. If they start dealing drugs or playing music too loud, the sheriff will be on their front porch. This is our neighborhood and you can't trash it ... Drug dealers have counted on us to be quiet. But we're fixing to run them out of the neighborhood."

Other groups you may be committed to might include alumni associations or organizations you were involved with in the past. Sometimes people graduate out of a group and yet can be involved and supportive of junior members as they come along.

There are several age specific organizations such as scouting, Active 20-30 International and the Junior League which need assistance from those who have graduated out of the age brackets.

None of us can be supportive of every cause. Part of the challenge is finding causes which provide the greatest meaning and value to you, causes into which you can put your heart and financial support.

A commitment to one group may mean saying no to another. So choose your causes carefully. Be sure you are making the best use of your personal resources. Often the most important contribution is your time.

It is also important to recognize that at certain times you outgrow a group. Your interests change, their focus changes. Recognize it is time to move on — let the reins pass to others. Some people hang on and on and on, long after they have given what they have to contribute. Give up a spot for new blood, freeing you to find another group to join and serve.

For this reason, some organizations have a maximum time one may serve as an officer or director, to ensure opening up room for new leadership and allowing leaders the chance to explore new opportunities.

Quality of Life: Community

> **A community is like a ship; everyone ought to be prepared to take the helm.**
> **— Henrik Ibsen**

While communities must have leaders, a quality community rotates the job of leaders and followers. Certainly all cannot be leaders and followers simultaneously. But over a period of time, every person should have the opportunity to serve in the roles required for communities to exist, co-exist and continue.

A true community is a safe place. It is where you can literally spill your guts, cry, laugh, and enjoy knowing the sharing of your experiences will remain safe and secure, even confidential, if need be.

In talking to a friend, I commented that very shortly he would be celebrating a birthday. Now that Dan is over 50, he responded, "The only birthday I care to recognize and celebrate anymore is the anniversary of my remaining off the bottle." As an Alcoholics Anonymous member, he celebrates his new found life with freedom from alcoholism. His community of AA means more to him than the commemoration of another year of life. Dan has told me he would not be alive today were it not for his commitment and the commitment of his community to support him through his trying times.

> In Alcoholics Anonymous, Dan has found a haven of safety, comfort and consolation. With other recovering alcoholics he was encouraged to share his story, tell about his drinking and be comforted in knowing he was not alone.

To maintain confidentiality, only first names are used and there is no desire or attempt to identify people outside the context of the AA meeting. Where they work or what they do is not connected with the reason for their being together in this community. They are there because of the desire to take each day one day at a time, working towards remaining free of the addiction to alcohol.

AA is a community which requires the confession of brokenness and the same is true of many other communities. Until you have confessed and acknowledged your brokenness, you are not able to become whole again. The reality is that every human being is broken and vulnerable. We have tenderness, softness — hurts that require support to be nurtured back to good health.

> **Too many times for comfort I have expected to reap good when I know I have sown evil . . . I try to plant peace if I do not want discord; to plant loyalty and honesty if I want to avoid betrayal and lies.**
>
> **— Maya Angelou**

Returning to our bank deposit analogy, within communities, one time you may be sharing your depression, hurts or wounds and later you may be the nurturing, caring party. If you want others to care, you must care; if you want to be honestly challenged, be ready to honestly challenge.

> Just as schools and sports teams have a spirit, within most communities there is a spirit. It may not be totally understood, but it can be seen, it can be felt and it is known. The idea of community

Quality of Life: Community

spirit, about your hometown, your home team, your home neighborhood is part of the bonding together of kindred spirits. This is the essence of belonging. That the group is as important to you as you are to them — a feeling of pride in the connection.

Do you recall the P.O.W. bracelets worn during the Vietnam War in support of our prisoners of war, or the yellow ribbons many wore while waiting for the release of the Iranian hostages and later for the safe return of our troops from the Gulf War? Now there are red ribbons for those who support AIDS victims. These personal decorations create a feeling of community between the wearers — an instant connection.

In his book, *The Different Drum: Community Making and Peace*, M. Scott Peck, M.D., states that "the spirit of true community is inevitably the spirit of peace and love." He explains that even agnostic and atheist members generally report a community-building workshop as a spiritual experience. The Christian understanding of community incorporates the spirit of peace and love created by the group, as well as, experiencing the presence of the divine spirit.

A community develops when there is the willingness to practice the love, discipline and sacrifice required for the blending of diverse individuals into a functioning body.

Communities afford their members a freedom of expression, the opportunity to gain wisdom, to share wisdom and to grow and prosper through the sharing and the togetherness.

In this age of rapidly growing technology with a world undergoing radical transformation, the challenge involves an ever expanding community.

Positive social change is linked to personal transformation and so, while we are actively serving our families and communities, we are also attending to our own personal needs.

Challenging all of us in the years ahead is the need to build a global community that includes all of humanity with the emphasis on the essence of the human spirit in an interconnected global environment.

My wish for you is that you will choose, participate in, and appreciate the *many* communities of your life.

In finding the communities that will impact your quality of life, you will be adding to the current of others doing the same. Together we may just change the world.

 Chapter 3

Education — A Never-Ending Quest

The more you know, the more you realize how much more there is to learn.

When you think of education, you probably think of conventional schooling such as nursery school, grade school, high school and college.

However, education takes many forms, both formal and informal. Learning starts at birth and continues until death. It happens in many places and ways — sometimes when least expected.

Education is not preparation for life; education is life itself.
— **John Dewey**

There is a need to develop a larger concept of education. Every activity produces a lesson. Every person is a teacher. Every place is a schoolroom. The universe is your university.

You are regularly bombarded with words, voices and pictures. It is important to be very selective in what you read, watch and hear. Certainly diversions for simple relaxation and enjoyment are in order. Nevertheless, a portion of your time should be devoted to keeping current with events in your world or to further your standing in life through education.

The mind, once expanded to the dimensions of larger ideas, never returns to its original size.
— Oliver W. Holmes

Seldom is there only one way to solve a problem — be receptive to new ideas and different approaches.

Part of the value of education is learning to keep your peripheral antenna extended to hear, consider and evaluate the many choices presenting themselves.

Education can and should be on-going and never-ending.

Quality of Life: Education

We can take inspiration from Michelangelo, who created unsurpassed works of art and yet, in his ninetieth year, regretted that he must die just when he was beginning to learn the rudiments of being an artist.

When the student is ready, the teacher will appear.
— Chinese Proverb

That teacher may have any one of many different titles — mentor, boss, parent, child, friend or relative

Many are lucky enough to have had at least one teacher who saw something special in us and by encouraging us, significantly altered our lives.

As humorous speaker, Roger Masquelier told me, "Many people have affected my life, but one memorable woman, Vinnie Knappenberger, my 12th grade English teacher, made me realize that I was a real person with something to give my peers. I was a complete nonentity in elementary school, and she once told me I had a talent for writing. I think it changed my life."

Others receive life changing inspirations and guidance from things they have read or seen.

Fellow speaker, Dorothy "Dottie" Walters once told me about the time her friends were going on to college and she was unable to join them because she needed to work two jobs to support herself and her mother. "I was reading Amelia Earhart's biography at that time, and found a great pearl of thought in it. This is what she told me:

'Some of us have great runways already built for us.
If you have one. Take off!

If you don't have one, then realize that it is your responsibility
To grab a shovel and BUILD ONE for yourself.
and for all those who will come on after you.'

"I hope my life will be seen as full of the construction of runways — and that people might remember that whenever I got knocked down, that I got up again."

We just must not, we just cannot afford the great waste that comes from neglect of a single child.
— Lyndon Johnson

Involvement in your children's education is one of the finest gifts you can give them. Not only do your children learn what you explicitly teach them, they also learn by observing the way you live — your attitudes, prejudices, thoughts, feelings, likes and dislikes.

While Gilbert and Virginia fully supported formal education for their two daughters, Elizabeth and Darcy, they thought nothing of occassionally taking the girls out of school for some "real life" education.

Once, while living in the Midwest, a series of excursions were planned. First, the girls watched as a farmer's field was being prepared for planting. They returned later to see the seed being sown, weekly observed the small shoots turn into mature wheat plants, and then watched as the wheat was harvested.

Quality of Life: Education

Next, they visited a silo to see how the wheat was stored and a flour mill to view the grain turned into flour. The last stop was a bakery where they saw bread made and were able to sample the aromatic, freshly baked product. "I can't eat a slice of bread without thinking about all the work involved in turning those little seeds into a loaf of bread," Elizabeth said. "I've always been grateful to my parents for providing us with this unique learning experience."

Children are impressionable and have fewer inhibitions. They tend to maintain a positive and unbaised outlook. Given the opportunity, most children want to learn. Often it isn't until they are taught to behave otherwise by their peers, parents and even teachers, that learning becomes more of a chore or requirement than a fun and fulfilling experience.

Katherine recalls a high school English class as one of her favorites, until one day her teacher arrived, and with an uncharacteristic and toneless voice announced to the class they were going to *have* to study poetry. The teacher then proceeded to explain why poetry wasn't fun or exciting to *her*. To this day, those feelings conveyed by her teacher are stronger in Katherine's mind than any one poem the class ever discussed.

Education gives greater enjoyment to life through increased ability to appreciate and understand. A broad liberal education requires students to study subjects they may not have chosen voluntarily, such as arts and literature.

This will not necessarily make an art connoisseur or music aficionado of the casually informed. However, it may permit enjoyment and appreciation by virtue of providing background information.

Life often deals with nuances and subtleties. It is important to know the differences between choices of words that may be used to express thoughts and ideas, not only to understand but also to effectively speak and write.

While knowledge and education may not change the way you look, it will change the way you look at the world.

> **Our progress as a nation can be no swifter than our progress in education. The human mind is our fundamental resource.**
> **— John F. Kennedy**

Educated people generally have more and better employment opportunities. A college graduate will take home nearly a half million dollars more than a high school graduate over the span of an average career. It is almost impossible to support any kind of meaningful lifestyle on the minimum wage jobs typically available to the under-educated.

Quality of Life: Education

Increased mechanization has replaced many of the routine manual labor jobs in factories, mines and on farms which were previously available to the uneducated. More and more entry-level positions require greater skills, not less.

> **If you think education is expensive, try ignorance.**
> **— Derek Bok, Harvard President**

The statistical correlation between high school dropouts and criminals is shocking. Approximately 80% of prison inmates in the United States are high school dropouts. Many see the school dropout rate as an underlying cause for the rise in criminal behavior.

> Isn't it amazing that we are willing to pay anywhere from $15,000 to $40,000 a year to keep a single individual in prison, but less than $6,000 a year to keep a child in school?

The cost of housing and funding inmates does not include the peripheral costs such as those taken on by an inmate's family, both financial and emotional; costs to the crime victim and society at large; and costs to capture and convict. There is also the loss of taxes that would have been contributed by the now-incarcerated, potential wage earner.

> **You are more likely to go to prison if you dropout than to die from cancer if you smoke.**
> **— Randy Lewis, spokesman for the Florida Department of Education.**

Of course, the lack of education isn't the only contributing factor to criminal activity. However, education can be the key to diverting some youngsters from a life of crime.

An inadequate education also contributes to the number of people living on public assistance. More than half of the nation's welfare families are headed by a dropout.

> A person on a payroll is a taxpayer and a contributing citizen. A person not on a private payroll, often joins the public dole, to be supported by all of us.

Fortunately, not all high school dropouts turn to lives of crime and public assistance.

My son, Hal, dropped out of high school. He left school because he was not a good student, partly because he was in a poor educational environment.

But more importantly, he dropped out because he liked his job as a meat cutter. He would much rather be cutting meat and serving customers than be in the classroom. Hal had a smile on his face and took pride in his work.

Later he became a truck driver. He talked about his job and his truck with enthusiasm and delight. It was very evident he thoroughly enjoyed what he was doing.

In both cases, Hal discovered what he had to learn to be happy and so he was successful. It is far more important that a

Quality of Life: Education

person be a happy meat cutter or truck driver than a frustrated, educated fool.

When we are educated sufficiently to perform the job we love, odds are we are going to have a better, well-adjusted life.

There are many who do not adapt to conventional educational environments or who have limited abilities to learn in formal classroom activities. This certainly need not preclude their continuing to learn.

Education means developing the mind, not stuffing the memory.
— Anonymous

Correspondence courses are available on almost every conceivable subject, but there is something to be said about having a classroom teacher who assigns, comments, corrects and returns homework.

It takes someone truly dedicated and motivated to stay with a correspondence course from beginning to end. Those who have done so are to be commended for working to increase their education on their own.

Trade schools are an excellent way to learn specific job skills. The major drawback is they do not provide the well-rounded education of a college or university. Some see this as a plus. They can learn the necessary job skills of a trade in a relatively short period of time and quickly be on the job earning a living.

Although not as prevalent in modern times, some trades can still be learned through apprenticeships. For those unsure if a specific trade is appropriate for them, volunteering can also offer insight.

Some high schools and universities offer co-operative education which allows students to earn credits toward graduation by working in their chosen field. A co-op also gives students the chance to discover if they have selected the right major.

Many high schools and colleges offer evening and weekend programs as well as classes during the day. In addition, almost all universities and colleges offer continuing education or extended studies courses. These programs allow individuals to continue their education in a more formal setting without having to go through the actual college admission process.

Courses can cover a wide range of subjects from basic skills in English composition or computer use to more in-depth studies of a particular writer or literary topic. Some colleges also use extended studies to cover more technical, business-oriented topics such as grant writing and designing a business plan which typically do not find places in the standard conventional classroom setting.

For the older, returning student, there are a multitude of support programs to make the transition back to school easier.

"When I decided to return to college to earn my business degree, I was really apprehensive. I thought I'd be uncomfortable with the younger students, but nothing could have been further from the truth," Louise told me. "Everyone was friendly and

cooperative — both students and professors. In fact, some of the professors mentioned that they preferred older students who were more apt to be there because they really wanted to learn. I was also surprised by how many other returning students there were — housewives whose children had grown, retired military personnel looking for a second career, and others like me. I was a divorced mother looking to education to provide me with a means of supporting my family. I know I got more out of my education because I was able to bring with me some 'real life' experience."

Professionals need to stay on the leading edge of new developments in their fields. Many, such as lawyers and accountants, are required to participate in continuing education for license renewal or to keep certificates active.

Continuing education credits can be earned through attending seminars and college classes. Some professional and trade organizations offer credits for attendance at monthly meetings where an hour long speech on a topic of interest is presented. Many of these meetings are open to the public and are promoted through newspaper and television bulletin boards.

There are many other opportunities for formal learning above and beyond the classroom. Some of the alternatives include video instruction and audio tapes which can be listened to repetitively while driving, walking or jogging.

When was the last time you wandered around a really good book store? Weren't you amazed by the wealth and variety of available information?

If you haven't visited a public library lately, you may be surprised at how libraries have evolved. Yes, there are still lots of books — fiction, non-fiction, reference, and so on. But you are also likely to find microfilm and computers.

Microfilm makes old newspapers and magazines readily available. Can you imagine the storage room that would be required if it wasn't for microfilm?

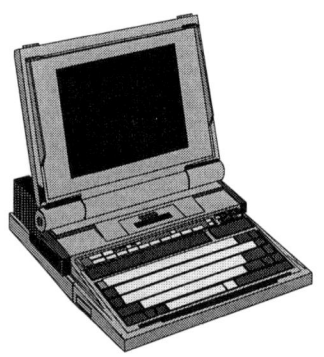

Computers have become wonderful educational tools. A complete set of encyclopedias can be stored on a compact disc. Not only does this make updating information more convenient, these discs have the capability to include audio. Look up Winston Churchill and you get not only pictures and text, but you can also hear his speeches. Or if you need to know the pronunciation of a word, look it up and along with the definition, today's compact disc dictionaries can provide you with an audio recording of the word being spoken. Look up lion and hear it roar!

Computers offer more learning opportunities through bulletin boards and information services such as PRODIGY® and CompuServe® which can be accessed by modem.

Quality of Life: Education

Magazines are published covering almost any conceivable subject from *Accounting Today* to *Zoo News*. In addition to general interest magazines found on most newsstands, many special interest groups and professional and trade organizations publish magazines and newsletters addressing specific concerns.

Television, particularly public television, offers wonderful opportunities to encounter entertaining learning experiences. Two channels available to television viewers are The Learning Channel and The Discovery Channel.

Knowledge is power and lifelong learning truly is the path to a better life. These networks are highly valued resources to millions of people.
— Dr. Harold E. Morse,
Chairman and CEO of
The Learning Channel

Our daily newspaper provides us with information on current events, along with sports, how-to columns, advice to the lovelorn, births, deaths, marriages, recipes, editorials, letters to the editor, entertainment news, comics, calendars of events, classifieds and advertisements.

Technology also holds the key to our learning future. Companies are currently developing a number of educational tools which will take advantage of the ever-growing number of new forms of interactive communication. Television systems within the classroom are being updated to allow for two-way communication with live images and sounds being beamed simultaneously to and from two separate locations. These types of

classes will allow students to attend classes at far away universities by simply meeting in a local classroom or even by direct hook up in their homes.

> Education and knowledge can sometimes increase by just letting your mind wander. It is amazing what brilliant ideas may occur in a creative setting!

I've discovered that simply wondering and inquiring about things helps to inform and add to my education.

It is amazing how and when information, thoughts and ideas will occur. I regularly carry a notebook, have note paper next to my bed, in my car or wherever I may be, so the fleeting thoughts can be captured before they escape.

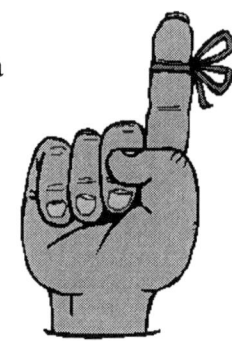

Sometimes it may be necessary to use a memory jogger because it may not be possible or appropriate to make a note when a thought occurs to you.

For example, in church or a darkened theater, it could be something said by the speaker or shown on the screen which prompts an idea.

When I think about something I want to remember and am unable to record the particulars, I place my watch on the other wrist. This creates such a disturbing feeling that I know something is wrong and invariably I can recall my thought.

Quality of Life: Education 71

There have been times in the past when I have had two thoughts occur to me and I was unable to capture either one on paper. After putting my watch on the other wrist, I moved a ring from one finger to another as a reinforcement.

> **He who asks a question is a fool for five minutes,**
> **he who does not ask a question is a fool forever.**
> **— Chinese Proverb**

I remember being a curious and questioning child while in grade school. One time I returned to visit my former 6th grade teacher and started asking questions. She replied, "You are just as nosy now as you were in school!"

Possibly some of my inquisitiveness has bordered on nosiness. On the other hand if you don't ask, you are not likely to learn.

> Many people need to create the proper environment for learning. That environment may be a secluded location or a quiet time, possibly away from home rather than a conventional study hall or library.

This is very true of a friend of mine. Rachel says, "While in college I wrote some of my best papers and did some of my best research by packing up all my books, notes and materials, checking into a local hotel for the weekend and turning the room into a mini-library. I could never write in my own room while living in the dorms. Even in high school I did something similar. I would choose a room in the house where I was going to do my

writing or research and then no one was allowed in or out until I had accomplished my goals for that day."

> **An education isn't how much you have committed to memory, or even how much you know. It's being able to differentiate between what you do know and what you don't. It's knowing where to go to find out what you need to know; and it's knowing how to use the information once you get it.**
> **— William Feather**

I once read that everything there is to know is doubling every seven years. The speed at which knowledge is developing and the world is changing, makes the continuous journey of education significant to all of us.

> **Let us think of education as the means of developing our greatest abilities, because in each of us, there is a private hope and dream which, fulfilled can be translated into benefit for everyone and greater strength for our nation.**
> **— John F. Kennedy**

Chapter 4

Career — Love What You Do; Do What You Love

Jack Lemmon, the actor, recently stated that like many people, he once thought success meant having money or fame and that having fame or money would end all his troubles.

Now he says, "It doesn't. The problems just change. With money and fame you get new problems just as big."

He adds, "A man who sweeps streets can be a success . . . if he loves what he's doing, and he does it as well as he possibly can."

Many people question how they can find a career doing what they love to do.

And that is the point of this chapter — getting you to think about what you love to do and to learn how to evaluate career opportunities.

It may surprise you to learn many people do not really know what they enjoy doing. Young people often spend more time discussing what movie to see on Saturday night than they do examining the type of profession or career to enter.

Just think about the first time you looked for a new job. Did you spend much time analyzing your skills, your talents and the things you enjoy doing, or did you just scan the want ads for a job you thought you could do? Many people stay in the jobs they "fall into" for many years, some even for a lifetime.

While just "any job" may do for after school or summer work, more consideration needs to be given in seeking your lifetime careers.

Do you consider your work a "calling"? Do you have a passion for it? Or is it "just" a job?

Find something you really like to do and you'll never have to work a day in your life.
— Harvey Mackay

If you won the lottery tomorrow, would you continue in the same job? Or would you do something entirely different? What would you do?

Quality of Life: Career

A few lucky people know from an early age what they want to be when they grow up. Their choice was probably influenced by a parent, teacher or some significant event. We sometimes read of performers bitten by the acting bug while in school or writers who completed their first novel before the age of ten.

Some follow in their parents' footsteps or inherit control of the family business.

This story of Gerald and Cory Smith offers a bit of a twist to the usual father and son business story.

Gerald had wanted to become an attorney, but was unable to pass the bar exam. He sat for it several times, sometimes coming very close — but never quite succeeding.

In the course of time, Gerald had a son, Cory, who went to college and did become an attorney.

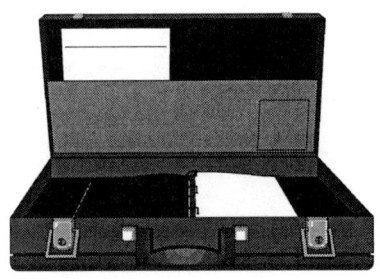

The accomplishment of his son seemed to provide the necessary drive for Gerald to make the commitment to study harder. The next time the exam was given, he succeeded in passing. Gerald and Cory established a law firm containing both of their names. In this case the first "Smith" in "Smith & Smith" was really that of the son rather than the father.

Many people complete college with a specific career in mind, yet within five years find themselves in a different field. That is one of the reasons it is preferable to obtain a broad-based education which will prepare a student for life rather than a particular job.

For those still unable to make a career choice, there are career counselors who can help you identify your likes, dislikes, strengths and weaknesses. These counselors can help point you in the right direction in setting career objectives.

The Myers-Briggs Type Indicator® (MBTI®) can be extremely useful in career guidance and in counseling as to jobs which will give the greatest satisfaction. Aptitude is, of course, also a key factor. One of the original purposes for developing the MBTI was to help individuals during World War II to find work at which they would be productive and successful. Isabell Briggs-Myers believed, ". . . one of the most important motivations for career choice is a desire for work that is intrinsically interesting and satisfying and that will permit use of preferred function and attitudes, with relatively little need for using less-preferred processes."

In *Using the Myers-Briggs Type Indicator in Organizations,* Sandra Krebs Hirsh talks about matching natural preference with the demands of work or the work environment. At that point individuals will generally feel more satisfied with the tasks and meaning provided by the work. When there is a mismatch between type and occupation, people frequently report feeling tired and inadequate. Additionally, when people are miscast in terms of doing work not aligned with their preferences,

Quality of Life: Career

the work product is less likely to supply the same level of quality as when the preferred preferences of the individual are utilized.

A job consisting of repetitive activities which would be considered boring by some may be satisfying to others who would be frustrated by a job involving a variety of tasks.

Some people work best in a large bureaucratic, governmental type of environment, enjoying themselves and functioning well. Others may be entrepreneurial-oriented or work most effectively in a smaller, less structured office.

There are people-oriented extroverts who would probably be happier in a service type business and introverts who may find research to be their cup of tea.

Some enjoy working at a desk while others would feel claustrophobic if they couldn't work out-of-doors. Some thrive on physical activity and others don't want to push anything more than a pencil.

> **There are few failures among people who have found work they like enough to do well.**
> **— Clarence E. Flynn**

An important part of setting career objectives is finding the niche or niches which are personally most satisfying to you.

A parable about careers and life states, "You make a living by what you get, but you make a life by what you give."

In his book *Super Joy: In Love With Living*, psychologist Paul Pearsall, Ph.D., tells a story that says a lot about personal perspectives on work.

One day, while he was home working at his word processor, Pearsall was interrupted by a loud buzzing noise. He stepped outside and found that his septic tank was being cleaned.

Three workmen standing by a large truck watched as hoses vacuumed the system.

As Pearsall approached the men, one of them said, "Well, Doc, how would you like to be doing this all day? Some job, eh?"

Then the second worker said, "This isn't so bad. I'm getting decent money, so I can send my daughters to college. Every day working is a day for them in college."

The third man looked up from adjusting a valve on the truck and said, "We have to keep a better eye on the pressure. We don't want any fumes escaping. You know, this work saves the environment. None of these homes could be here if we didn't have this equipment and do this job. It's like a small thing, but at least I'm doing more than *talk* about a clean world. The good doctor couldn't live out here in the country and write his books if somebody didn't do this."

> These three men had exactly the same job. But they didn't have the same perspective on the work they did. Which view is most like yours?

As Dr. Pearsall writes, "Are you working because you have to, or because you're helping yourself and your family grow, or because you have a vision, a dream, some belief that what you are doing matters in the overall scheme of things?"

All three perspectives are important. Pearsall calls them the "Three D's of Work."

>First, is *DEMAND* — You must balance what you demand from the world with what you contribute to the world.
>
>Second is *DEVELOP* — you need to see yourself and your family enhanced by your efforts.
>
>Third, you must have a *DREAM* — A clear picture of your overall purpose and contribution to the world that goes beyond the everyday work routine.

As you balance the three perspectives, be sure to give sufficient thought to the last "D" — your dream — the meaningful vision of the purpose of your work. If you do, you will perform better and enjoy it more.

A great many people complain that their work is boring. The tendency is to blame the job for lack of challenge. What usually makes work drudgery, however, is one's attitude — not the work itself.

> **One of the reasons that I have had such a happy life is that I have always loved work as much as most people love hobbies.**
> **— Patricia Fripp, CSP, CPAE**

No task need be boring, for the simple reason that every job contains within it a hidden challenge — How can your job be done better?

> Your attitude determines your altitude. Do you want to fly high or just barely get off the ground? If you find your work boring or lacking in challenge, think about the following story.

Could anything be more boring than sweeping floors? Murray Spangler, a department store janitor in Canton, Ohio wasn't bored, even though the dust made him wheeze and cough. Many men would have given up and quit. Instead, Spangler set out to find a better way to clean floors.

"Why not eliminate the broom," he wondered, "Maybe something that would suck up dust . . .?"

Spangler's thinking led to a crude but workable vacuum cleaner, which he induced an old friend in the leather business to finance. The friend's name was H. W. Hoover.

> In work, as in life in general, the person who gets ahead is the one who does more than is necessary and keeps on doing it.

Quality of Life: Career

Danny Cox said the shortest and most effective motivational speech he ever received were the words, "We are looking for your replacement!"

Danny decided he wanted to keep his job. He improved his attitude and his performance improved accordingly.

An estimated 80% of all Americans are working at jobs they don't like, wouldn't choose if they had to do it all over again, and which they "will leave tomorrow if I win the lottery!"

Even being in a management position is not as wonderful as some people imagine it to be.

A survey completed by the National Institute of Business Management found that a third of all managers aren't happy with their current positions. More than three out of 10 mid-level managers are in touch with head-hunters actively looking for new jobs.

The reasons they give for seeking new work are: too much stress, personality conflicts with their bosses and lack of challenging work.

Some years ago a popular phrase stated, "America — Love it or leave it." The same can be said about the career or occupation in which you are now engaged. Give it your all, your full commitment and devotion, or find another job. You spend too much time in work-related activities not to enjoy them.

However, be cautious about changing employers. Your talents and abilities are typically known by your employer and in turn, you know what your company expects from you.

This doesn't necessarily mean devotion to your employer is absolute. Be open to other opportunities which might come along. Instead of making a hasty decision when a new opportunity presents itself, take your time. Fully explore your options before making a firm decision.

> You never know what the future holds. Your job can be yanked out from under you through no fault of your own in these days of volatile economics. You need to be prepared to consider and explore other opportunities whenever they may arise.

Sometimes fate causes a change in direction.

While working in an oil refinery, Ted had an accident which necessitated he be retrained for office work. Ted became proficient as a bookkeeper and knowledgeable in computers. But fate stepped in once again. Due to another unfortunate event, he was significantly disabled and is now preparing for career options with the impaired dexterity of his hands, arms and legs.

> **All limitations are self-imposed . . . It's not what happens to you in life, it's what you do about it.**
> **— W. Mitchell, CPAE**

Quality of Life: Career

A young man was asked, "Are you looking for work?" He replied, "Not necessarily, but I would like a steady paycheck."

Too many people are working just for the money, and not realizing the enjoyment and fulfillment a career can provide.

It is regrettable but true that some people spend twenty or thirty years working at a job they dislike. Later, after they are turned out to pasture and have received their gold watch, they embark upon their true passion. Unfortunately, at this stage of life they may be too old to enjoy or too rigid to meet the needs of a new situation.

If you are one who is unfullfilled in his or her current career, why not change? Are you truly stuck and unable to leave your present position? Think about it.

While some career changes may just require taking a chance, other changes may mean a return to school. Because of economics it may take a long time to complete your preparation. However, if you really want it, you can do it. There is very little in life that cannot be achieved if you are willing to make the commitment, and have the drive and willingness to do what is required.

Whatever the mind can conceive and believe, it can achieve.
— **Napoleon Hill**

I have known two men who spent many years preparing to become registered nurses. Each was engaged in that caring

profession for some time. Oddly enough, both aspired to become Certified Public Accountants.

Robert, the older of the two, made the transition and worked in the field of finance for the balance of his career, enjoying it very much and finding it quite fulfilling.

Ken has passed the CPA examination but has not yet completed the experience requirement necessary to receive certification.

In both situations, the individuals were married and had children. It took significant commitment, sacrifice and perseverance on the part of the entire family for the man of the household to continue in the nursing profession while studying for a new career.

There are many stories of people who recognize their chosen occupation is not as satisfying to them as another might be.

While vacationing, I met Jeff Grandy, a Yosemite sales clerk and photographer, who was a trained mechanical engineer. Jeff told me this story about why he changed careers.

"When I was in fourth grade, we practiced air-raid drills. About this time I read the book, *Hiroshima!* Then along came the Bay of Pigs and then the Cuban missile crisis. All this served to jam the uncertainty and fear of the nuclear age in my head so hard it's never left. I was too young to fully comprehend all of it, but I knew I was scared and I knew it was evil spreading somehow.

"Ironically, years later, I built nuclear submarines for a living. At one point, I worked on the Trident, the world's most sophisticated nuclear submarine. One day I worked all day in the missile tube of this ship. By the end of the day, I was feeling the same fears I had as a kid, that this was an integral piece of some greater evil. I left the trade two months later, but fourteen years later, those fears still come back in dreams. I suppose my photography, which always focuses on the positive, has become over the years, a counterbalance for these feelings."

Because his current position was realtively low paying, I asked Jeff what he did when he needed both food and film, but didn't have money for both. He replied, "Well of course I ate a lot of rice until payday, and with my one precious roll of film tried to fully appreciate each picture I took. *Life's always a balancing act!*"

Whether you're thinking of making a change or looking for your first real job, there are several factors you should consider when comparing employers.

Quality employers find there is much to be gained by sharing credit for success. Good management involves other important items like . . .

— recognizing latent abilities and giving them a chance to develop,

— asking opinions and advice instead of just telling people to do things,

— a pat on the back when the going is rough,

— passing the credit for achievement along to everyone who had a part in it,

— appreciation for effort.

These intangible attributes and others can be termed "psychic income."

Psychic income is very important to some. This term can cover everything from a plush office with a window view to working in a glamorous profession where you may rub elbows with celebrities to co-workers who are friendly and helpful.

Psychic income is that non-monetary boost you get from your job.

Linda worked for two years at what she terms a "sick company." "I really loved my work — it was challenging and interesting and I was very good at it. This company had real problems in my department before I came on board. They were over six months behind in their work. Nothing had been filed for years, so a lot of time was wasted just looking for information."

She put a lot into her job — worked extra hours and managed to get the department cleaned up and the work current. "But my efforts were never appreciated. No matter what I did, it was never enough. There was no spirit of

Quality of Life: Career

cooperation. Backstabbing was rampant and was actually encouraged by the owners. It was a very demoralizing atmosphere. I finally realized I was becoming as nasty as the people with whom I worked. No matter how much I loved the work, I had to get out of there."

Linda now does work she enjoys in a company where her efforts are appreciated. "I enjoy going to work again. My attitude has completely turned around."

You may want to consider how understanding the company is towards such things as providing time off during the work day to attend school plays or parent-teacher conferences.

And a company reputation can mean a lot to you. Does the company treat its employees, customers and vendors fairly? Or is it known as a company with rapid employee turnover, or numerous customer complaints regarding poor service and shoddy goods?

Are vendors paid timely? Not only can certain business tactics point to a poorly run organization but also to company stability and ultimately your own job security.

Are you being hired at a high enough level where you can turn the company around and make a difference? And if so, will you have the support you need to do this?

Other people are concerned with environmental issues. How does this company's policies and practices impact the environment?

What about community relations? How much does the company contribute back to the community in which it operates?

Another factor to consider is advancement opportunities. Unless, you are the boss' daughter or married to her, you will have to pay your dues before becoming the chairman of the board. Paying your dues often means taking on the grunge jobs nobody else wants. By doing these jobs well, you prove yourself capable of more challenging and responsible assignments.

A high school boy named Paul Potter visited the Sears Roebuck office on the west side of Chicago as part of a boy's club tour. He asked many questions, and the tour guide asked why he was so interested. "My father has a retail store," he replied, "and I thought maybe I could learn something that will help him."

The guide liked his response, and offered Paul a job on Saturdays. There were other jobs during the following years, part-time during the school week, and full-time during vacations. The jobs were in different retail departments, support departments, offices and finally sections of the Midwest headquarters.

This went on through high school and four years of college. Upon graduation he was invited to go on for an MBA on a Sears scholarship. Paul continued

Quality of Life: Career

working for Sears at increasingly higher levels ultimately retiring from an executive position.

> Paul never received a check other than the trademark green vouchers from Sears, but he recalled, "I never had a dull day on my job in 40 years."

Judging employers strictly on monetary compensation can be a mistake. Your prospective employer may well expect longer hours for higher pay. Be sure that you are willing to devote more time to your work which may mean less time for your family and leisure activities.

Compare retirement plans. A smaller paycheck now may well be worth a much larger paycheck after you retire. Some companies also offer stock options or the ability to purchase company stock at below market price.

What about insurance? Compare coverage as well as deductibles. And don't forget vacations, holidays and bonuses.

Fortunately, more and more people, when they discover they are in the wrong career, are willing and able to change their occupations. This may take years of night study or sacrifices to learn new skills. But it is worth it.

You spend too much of your time at work not to be enjoying what you are doing. Your personality, temperament and aptitude should be directed in the areas of personal fulfillment and enjoyment.

The quality of a man's life is in direct proportion to his commitment to excellence, regardless of his chosen field of endeavor.

— Vince Lombardi

Chapter 5

Finances — To Achieve Financial Independence, Start Early!

What will you do when you win the lottery?

Seriously, think about this. What would you do if you had an unlimited supply of financial resources — how would your life be different?

In what ways would you spend more, save more, invest more? How would your friendships be modified? Would those of old still be with you? Would you suddenly acquire new friends as a result of your new found wealth?

Of course, there is one necessary prerequisite. So far, no one has yet won the lottery without buying at least *one* ticket.

Day dreaming or fantasizing about lottery winnings, if we are at all serious, has to be tied in with making the necessary expenditure.

Now mind you, I am not advocating gambling. I am just using this to illustrate the difference between fantasy dreams and reality dreams.

Even if you do buy a lottery ticket, the odds are stacked so much against you that you better not count on winning to assure your future financial security.

Instead, let's see what you can do while traveling along life's journey so as to be financially well off when you reach your selected retirement age.

Lack of money is the root of all evil.
— George Bernard Shaw

How much money do you *have*? How much do you *want*? How much do you *need* to live at the level you consider comfortable? How is your financial health? Is your wealth increasing, decreasing, or are you holding steady?

The best way to answer the last two questions is to take a periodic "snapshot" of your financial position.

First make a list of all your assets. Your bank accounts, home, furniture, jewelry, investments, vehicles, retirement accounts, (don't forget the cash value of life insurance), and personal goods (clothes, dishes, books, etc.). Although your family, good health and education are also assets, only include your *financial* assets on this list.

Quality of Life: Finances

Next, assign a value for each asset. For the purpose of this calculation, the fair market value should be what you could reasonably expect to receive if the asset was sold. Make your best guess.

Now, do the same for your liabilities (no, you don't get to include your mother-in-law here). Include the mortgage on your home, credit card balances and any outstanding loans.

Finally, subtract the total of your liabilities from the total of your assets. The difference is your net worth. By doing this calculation every year or so, you can see if your net worth is increasing or decreasing.

> **If you don't change the direction you are going, you are probably going to get where you are headed.**
> — **Chinese Proverb**

Is your net worth increasing and is it increasing as rapidly as you want? Before you can answer that question, you need to decide what you want to achieve with your wealth.

> **Would you tell me, please, which way I ought to go from here?**
> **That depends a good deal on where you want to get to, said the Cat.**
> **I don't care where, said Alice.**
> **Then it doesn't matter which way you go, said the Cat.**
> — **Lewis Carroll**

Is your goal to send your children to college so that they can support you in your old age? Do you want to amass a fortune in order to leave a considerable estate for your heirs, or do you want to guarantee sufficient funds to support you throughout your lifetime?

The answer to these financial questions are personal to each of you. Only you can determine your ultimate goals and the extent of sacrifice you are willing to make to attain those goals. Some of these sacrifices might require "tough love" commitments on your part. These are not easy choices. However, I can provide you with various suggestions on how best to meet your goals.

Each of us approaches the task of handling money differently.

We are not all equally gifted in the ability to understand and manipulate numbers. Some people really look forward to receiving their bank statement each month and derive a true joy out of reconciling it to the penny, no less. Others will accumulate bank statements and open them only when and if they feel they have to.

Chris says, "If it's a thick envelope that comes from the bank, everything's okay. It contains the cancelled checks and the statement. On the other hand, a real thin envelope from the bank,

Quality of Life: Finances

could be a check which has been returned, an overdraft notice or something of more serious consequences."

Thus, while the thin envelope may have bad news, Chris opens and attends to it promptly. The larger envelope is set aside for some rainy day (which Chris hopes never arrives) for review, reconciliation or disposition.

While I am not in favor of waiting for rainy days to reconcile bank statements — it should be done upon receipt — if you do not have a real affinity for financial matters, make life simpler for yourself by engaging the assistance of an expert such as a Certified Public Accountant, an independent bookkeeper, tax advisor, or financial planner.

> Whatever your needs, there is someone who
> possesses the expertise, knowledge and capability
> to respond to those needs.

Choose to do those tasks which you can do well and which you enjoy. Tasks not meeting that criteria, can be delegated to others to the extent you can afford their services.

There are two ways to increase your net worth — decrease expenses or increase income. To some extent, your income and expenses are not within your control. Food is a good example. You will always have an expense for food. Whether you eat consistently at fine restaurants or raise your own meat and grow your own vegetables, there is an expense involved Another example is housing. You may live in a studio apartment or a multi-million dollar mansion. Whichever it is, you have rent or house payments and maintenance costs.

Although you cannot entirely eliminate food and housing expenses, there are steps you can take to reduce those costs.

Certified Financial Planner, John B. Kelly says, "Controlling your expenses is the biggest factor in balancing out your finances. This is where the choices are made. Choices you can control. We don't always have a choice on the income side. When we do it may be that 1) all the money in the world could not overcome the 'expense nut' or 2) we lose self esteem in realizing we have no real alternatives because of an increase or huge budget requirement which controls our thoughts. There is no more harsh task master than debt."

One of the saddest things about modern life is the number of people spending money they don't have, for things they don't want, to impress people they don't like.

Watch out for "keeping up with the Joneses" or anyone else for that matter. It is always possible they might have some hidden resources unknown to you. Or they may have hit a jackpot.

While you are trying to keep up with the Joneses, they may be going deeper and deeper into debt. Their increased indebtedness eventually will have a day of reckoning, be it a form of bankruptcy, a divorce because of conflict between the parties, or other emotional turmoil.

Some people may spend lavishly without apparent adequate resources, producing envy or jealousy. It could be they have simply refinanced their home or entered into a debt consolidation plan.

Quality of Life: Finances

Before spending your hard earned money, consider the following tips, traps and tidbits.

Dollars and sense should go together.

Are you trying to satisfy a champagne appetite on a beer budget? Habit patterns are more easily formed than modified. Twenty-one repetitions of almost any event creates a habit. That's wonderful if they are time saving, cost saving practices you are pleased about and enjoy. Unfortunately, the overspending habit is a hard one to break. It is much easier to have a more modest or conservative spending pattern and occasionally live it up.

For instance, at finer restaurants you have the opportunity to choose an appetizer, a dessert and beverages. Consider going to an elegant restaurant for the main course and returning home to enjoy your dessert.

> Kate and Jim enjoyed eating breakfast out every Sunday at a cost of about $15 a week. One day they realized that if they prepared a gourmet breakfast at home, they could save $400 a year. Investing that savings at 8% would give them $29,240 in 25 years.

Kate and Jim found it was a matter of choosing to save those dollars and letting them add up for something more significant which would provide greater value and enjoyment.

In somewhat the same vein, you may be one of those who periodically attend sporting, musical or theatrical events. If you go regularly, you may be willing to buy a less expensive seat in a less desirable location and occasionally splurge at special events for a better seat.

However, if your attendance at events of this type are rather infrequent, when you do go, treat yourself to the best seats you can afford. It would be disheartening to attend a first rate production and find that you are in a corner, behind a post or way up in the balcony.

You would remember the experience of *where* you were, far longer than what it was you went to see. If you buy the best seat you can afford, you undoubtedly will remember the production rather than the amount you paid for the ticket.

> When considering major or so called "big ticket" purchases, evaluate the differences in quality with life expectancy of the item being acquired.

You may think things which have a higher initial outlay cost more. Although that may be true in the short run, in the long run, they may actually cost less.

To help evaluate this decision, divide the cost by the reasonable life expectancy to find the approximate cost per year or per month. You may find the more expensive item actually costs less per year, if its life expectancy exceeds that of the cheaper item. Or you may find only a few dollars per month difference which may be compensated by lower repair and maintenance costs and fewer defects than the cheaper model. The more expensive item may perform more functions, some of which might not be needed and others which might be very desirable.

> The higher quality item will probably give you greater enjoyment, possibly a longer life and more trouble free usage.

Of course, the most expensive item may not always be the best way to go. Patty and Dave wanted to buy a coffee machine, but they couldn't quite agree on the model. Dave wanted one with an automatic shut-off which added quite a bit to the price. Patty felt that for less money they could buy the less expensive model and a separate timer, thereby eliminating some of the things that could go wrong with the coffee pot. In the long run, buying the cheaper item paid off because Dave now uses instant coffee so the machine is hardly ever used.

And a long life isn't always that enticing. When Sally was shopping for kitchen floor covering, the salesman listed among the features of a particular brand that it would last at least 20 years. Sally looked him in the eye and said, "Mister, I'm not going to want to sweep, mop and look at this floor daily for 20 years. Sell me something I will need to replace in ten!"

For really big ticket items, such as an automobile, it is prudent to consider the pros and cons of purchase versus lease. You can find experts who are adept in calculating the net results of the various alternatives.

With sales tax being a major factor in most states, consider for example the difference between leasing and purchasing a luxury car that costs $30,000.

The sales tax is computed based on the full sales price, due at the time of the purchase and is non-refundable, non-prorated and non-recoverable no matter how long you keep the vehicle.

A lease may provide for the sales tax to be calculated on the amount of each lease payment. Consequently, the total sales tax paid would not only be less, but the time over which it would be paid would be much longer. This also relates to the time value of money, which is discussed later in the chapter.

There are many other factors entering into lease versus purchase decisions which need to be considered. Examining the alternatives and making the choice that best fits your circumstances will help you obtain a higher quality of life.

Of course, before making any purchase, evaluate the trade-off between consumption and investment: That $15,000 boat which gets used only a few times, sits in someone's vacant lot or garage for 5 years, and then gets sold for $5,000 translates into a huge opportunity loss as compared with investing the money you would have spent on monthly payments in a conservative mutual fund growing at 8 to 10% a year.

> In reality, many choices between consumption and investment are also choices between short term consumption and the long term ability to choose between consumption or not. Those who do not plan for the future often end up with no choices as to how they live their later years because their early choices have precluded them from many later options which require financial capital.

There is certainly nothing wrong with coupon clipping, looking for two-for-one opportunities, discounts and sales. All merchants promote in various ways. Watching for bargains and comparison shopping can permit you to receive the most for the least. This sometimes requires a degree of patience and also a willingness of not needing to be "firstest" with the "mostest".

Ginny makes a game out of bargain hunting. "The less I pay for something, the greater the enjoyment I receive. I get a real kick out of finding just the blouse I want — on the clearance rack."

Buying later, you may obtain better quality, something more enjoyable and certainly more affordable. Do watch out for bargains. A purchase is not a bargain, if you do not really need or sincerely want it.

Often people emotionally justify a decision because the price was right. You know, if you can get elephants for $100 each, you might like to have two because the price is right, but what do you need with one, let alone two?

With something such as an elephant (as ridiculous as this example may be), is the *total* price a bargain when you look at only the initial investment? Buying an elephant is only part of the cost of such an animal.

Naturally, you will need to house, feed and care for it. The added peripheral costs may far exceed the initial cost and that needs to be reckoned with when considering "bargain" acquisitions.

Now that you've looked at decreasing expenses, what can you do to increase income?

If you've chosen your ancestors carefully, you may receive an inheritance when the darlings die off. However, don't forget that while you're waiting for rich Uncle Thaddeous to kick the bucket, he may be making a new will in favor of his sweet young nurse — the new Mrs. Uncle Thaddeous.

For those of us who don't have rich relatives to rely on, increasing income can become a matter of working more overtime or taking on a second job. However, the costs associated with these alternatives can sometimes outweigh the benefits. Not only are there economic costs such as childcare, transportation and an increased number of fast-food meals to consider, but also the psychological costs of less time for your family or leisure activities, as well as higher stress levels.

> These costs can be handled better if the extra income is needed for a defined period of time instead of indefinitely.

There are ways to increase income without incurring these costs. Approach your employer to see what you need to do to get that next raise — then do it. Turn your hobby into a business — craft projects can be sold in boutiques or at fairs, for example.

Many employment opportunities are now available for those who stay at home and work. A young mother may have a part-time function she can perform with a computer while the baby sleeps. She is still able to tend to the infant without having to hire outside help which offsets some of the benefit gained by working.

It is also very possible that both spouses may be gainfully employed within the home, using modern communication technologies such as computers, modems and fax machines. What an opportunity to control your life and freedom!

Quality of Life: Finances

Another way to increase income is through saving and investing.

Tithe for yourself as well as for your church.
— Ben Franklin

Didn't Ben have a wonderful philosophy? Do not pay the butcher, the baker and the candlestick maker first and save what is left. Rather, save ten percent off the top then spend what's left over. There is much more significance to the *habit* of regularly saving than the magnitude of your savings.

Too many people think, "I will start saving next month or next year when I can put away a large amount."

Well, *mañana* sometimes never arrives and the ability to put away a large amount also seldom arrives. If we have been in the habit of spending, then increased earnings will more likely result in increased spending rather than increased saving.

Whatever you have — spend less!
— Samuel Johnson

The youngest earner or saver, even a small child, can learn the habit of saving, whether it be pennies, nickels or dimes.

If you acquire the habit of regular saving and if it is commenced early and continued for a reasonably long period of time, you will probably amass a fortune sufficient to last throughout your life. It is not feasible to wait until 55 to plan to retire at 65!

The magic of compounding happens when money put into a savings account earns interest which increases the amount in your savings account — the principal (your cash investment) plus the interest continues to earn more interest.

How much interest is earned depends on several factors — the principal amount, the interest rate, how often the funds are compounded and how long funds are invested. As an example, say you have made a New Year's resolution to save $12,000 next year. Among the options available to you are putting $12,000 in your savings account, either at the beginning or end of the year or putting in $1,000 each month. Assuming an interest rate of 8.0%, how much will you have at the end of the year?

Timing	Amount Invested	Investment Value at End of the Year with 8.0% Interest Compounded		
		Monthly	Quarterly	Annually
Beginning of the Year	$12,000	$12,996	$12,974	$12,960
End of the Year	$12,000	$12,000	$12,000	$12,000
$1,000 at Beginning of Each Month	$12,000	$12,457	$12,447	$12,080

As the chart illustrates, the earlier you deposit and the more often the compounding, the greater the earnings.

This next chart depicts the various results which can be achieved given differing interest rates and time periods.
The results were obtained using the following assumptions:
1) $10,000 was invested 2) interest was compounded annually at the end of each year.

There are computers, calculators and tables that can help you figure out what your savings will be worth using various rates and time periods.

Interest Rate	Years Invested			
	10	20	30	40
5%	16,300	26,500	43,200	70,400
10%	25,900	67,300	174,500	452,600
15%	40,500	163,700	662,100	2,678,600

There is also a simple shortcut to determine how long it takes to double your money at a given interest rate using annual compounding. Simply divide 72 by the rate. If you want to know how long it would take to double $10,000 at 5.0%, divide 72 by 5 which equals 14.4 years. A glance at the chart above shows this to be about right.

Hand in hand with compounding is the time value of money concept. Would you rather get $5,000 today or would you prefer to receive that $5,000 next year? Of course, you would rather have it today. It is a simple matter to conclude that $5,000 to be received next year just isn't quite as valuable as $5,000 received today.

Present value is the value today of that $5,000 to be received next year and is determined by interest rates. As an example, if you could earn 8.0% interest, how much would you need to invest today to have $5,000 in one year? Using annual compounding, the answer is $4,630.

The important thing to remember is to set savings and investment goals.

Goals are like automobiles, they won't run themselves, except downhill.

Just as children are told, "After you clean up your room, you can watch TV . . ." or "As soon as you clean off your plate, you can have dessert . . ." we react positively to goals.

Goals motivate us much of the time. To be effective, goals need to be realistic and attainable within a reasonable time frame.

This is one reason why it is so difficult for a person in their twenties to think about saving for retirement in their sixties. That is so-o-o far in the future and so uncertain in many ways, that it is difficult to fully appreciate 40-year goals. After all that is twice as far in the future as they have yet lived.

It is unfortunate but true, that at age 65 when literally hundreds of thousands of dollars have gone through the hands of most people, very little has been retained for use in retirement years.

In fact, out of every 100 Americans who retired at the age of 65, only three are truly wealthy; ten

Quality of Life: Finances

others are sufficiently well off that they do not need to work; about sixty-four are just existing on Social Security, small pensions or additional supplemental income; and twenty-three are living below the poverty level.

What a tragedy to have worked so hard, and earned so much to have squandered or spent it so that little is available for the sunset years!

Financial planner, Bert Hughes, has this to say about starting a savings plan. "Whether they do it alone, hire a planner, buy some books, or a combination of all three, the important thing is that they start doing it when they are young. *Most people spend more time planning and implementing their vacation or their next purchase be it a stereo or a car than they do planning their future financial viability.*"

Saving can even be accomplished without consciously realizing you are doing so. You can arrange for a part of each paycheck to be deposited into a savings account before the final check reaches you.

If you anticipate receiving a large tax refund, put the refund check directly into savings. You will have a hard time spending money you don't see.

Christmas savings accounts illustrate how many are able to accumulate the funds they would like by saving throughout the year. A one year goal is a reasonable length of time and provides specific results at the end.

In determining your savings goals, you may find it effective to establish at least three separate accounts. The first account would be long-term savings for retirement. The second account would be the money you set aside for that "rainy day" — emergencies or long-term unemployment. The third account would be for short-term goals, such as a vacation or home improvement. By establishing separate accounts for separate purposes, you have earmarked those funds and should find it more difficult to dip into your emergency fund to pay for your tickets to Hawaii.

The separate accounts will also help you evaluate how best to invest those funds. You will want to put your emergency funds into an easily accessible account, such as bank savings, even though the earnings may be small. You are trading income for liquidity.

On the other hand, unless you are close to retirement age, you will want your retirement funds in long-term investments.

To many people, their home is their most notable asset and they look to that investment to provide a significant portion of their retirement resources.

A fully paid-for home can provide shelter with the minimum costs of upkeep and taxes. On the other hand, selling the family home after the children are grown and purchasing a smaller home sufficient for the husband and wife, can also provide additional cash to add to retirement funds.

Quality of Life: Finances

A home is a unique investment, since not only does it house your family, it also can provide significant tax savings. In addition, housing has traditionally increased in value over time.

Because of the tax savings involved, you can generally afford a house payment larger than what you would pay for rent. However, you do need to be sure that you have allocated resources for taxes, insurance and maintenance.

You can adjust the tax withholding from your paycheck to make the larger house payment. The Internal Revenue Service Form W-4, which you can get from your employer, has a worksheet to assist you in determining your new withholding.

How much you can pay for a home is determined by a number of factors including your income, your debts, interest rates, the down payment, and the type of loan you get. The deciding factor may not be so much the cost of the house, but rather the monthly payment.

As we've seen in just the past few years, interest rates can be very volatile and this can have the biggest effect on your payment. As an example, if you can afford a $1,000 monthly principal and interest payment, at 5% you can carry a $186,282 mortgage; at 15% you can carry only a $79,086 mortgage. (These calculations are based on a 30 year fixed rate loan.)

Costs associated with buying and selling a home such as broker fees, loan fees, pest control and other closing costs, to say nothing of moving expenses, are significant. For this reason, you should try to find a house that will satisfy your needs for as long as possible.

Sometimes you can find a smaller house in a nice neighborhood that is big enough for you now and has room for expansion as your family grows. Before doing any extensive remodeling, be sure to analyze the costs and benefits. If you end up with the fanciest house in the neighborhood, you probably will not be able to recoup the remodel costs when you sell.

Purchasing a home isn't always the best alternative. Those with jobs requiring frequent transfers may find they are better off investing in stocks and bonds with the cash they would be putting into continuously buying and selling homes. Another investment alternative would be to buy a house in the city in which they plan to retire and use that house as a rental. They obtain tax benefits and build up equity at the same time.

Investment alternatives are limitless and the important thing is that you choose the best course of action for yourself.

Investments and returns will vary based upon your age, financial resources and other factors. Obviously people in their 20s can and probably should take greater risk than those in their 50s or 60s, who have less time to make up losses. As a person ages, consistent returns are more important than the opportunity for greater gains.

Quality of Life: Finances

Investment Pyramid

```
                    COMMODITIES

                    TAX SHELTERS

              STAMPS, RARE COINS,
                 GOLD, SILVER,
            PRECIOUS STONES, MANAGED
                  COMMODITIES

              EXPLORATORY DRILLING
             REAL ESTATE DEVELOPMENT

            RAW LAND VENTURE CAPITAL,
         DEVELOPMENT DRILLING, STOCK OPTIONS

         INDIVIDUAL STOCK TRADING ACCOUNTS,
              OIL & GAS INCOME FUNDS,
          MANAGED REAL ESTATE PROGRAMS,
              OPTION INCOME PROGRAMS

          DISCOUNT & CONVERTIBLE BONDS,
       GROWTH MUTUAL FUNDS, VARIABLE ANNUITIES,
              NET LEASED REAL ESTATE

    HIGH QUALITY INCOME SECURITIES, MUNICIPAL BONDS,
      LONG TERM GOVERNMENT BONDS, PERSONAL PROPERTY

         FIXED ANNUITIES, MUNICIPAL BOND FUNDS,
       TREASURY NOTES & BILLS, PERSONAL RESIDENCE

      SAVINGS CERTIFICATES, SAVINGS & LOAN ACCOUNTS,
       MONEY MARKET INSTRUMENTS, MONEY MARKET FUNDS

       LOCK BOX, CASH, CASH VALUE OF LIFE INSURANCE,
    PASSBOOK SAVINGS, SERIES E AND H BONDS, INSURED MUNICIPALS,
                    CHECKING ACCOUNTS
```

You need to prudently manage your funds. Evaluate to determine if you are obtaining an adequate and appropriate return on your invested dollars.

What are the yields? What are the associated risks? I would far rather get a consistent and reasonable yield than seek only the highs and extraordinary opportunities.

The Investment Pyramid on the previous page demonstrates the relationship of risk to returns. The investments on the bottom of the pyramid are very low risk, with associated lower earnings. As you go up the pyramid, the potential for greater earnings increases, as do the potential investment risks. The secret to optimizing return and minimizing risk is diversification.

Another factor to consider is inflation. Bert Hughes uses the analogy of high blood pressure versus the flu. "Stock market variations and interest rate movement are like the flu. Inflation is like high blood pressure: Painless in the short term but deadly over time."

Inflation decreases the spending power tomorrow of the dollar you saved today. If the interest earned on an investment is 8%, but the inflation rate is 5%, you have only actually gained 3% on your investment. Let's say you have decided you will need $50,000 a year to live comfortably after you retire and have made contributions to your savings based on this amount. However, because of the ravages of inflation, when you retire, that $50,000 a year may only be worth $30,000 a year in today's dollars.

Like you, I don't have a crystal ball and have no idea how accurate the above example may be. That is why you need to review your retirement needs and goals on a regular basis. A prudent decision made today may be a foolish course of action in ten years.

Much more can be said about financial affairs, but the essence is, do you sleep well and comfortably at night? Do you worry about your investments or do you relax and enjoy them because they are quality investments?

Risk is part of our daily lives. In addition to the financial risks associated with your investments, there are also a plethora of risk management tools available to insulate us from the trials and tribulations of everyday living.

Some of these tools are just common sense, like looking both ways before you cross the street, or eating healthy foods and getting plenty of exercise, or staying out of dark alleys and biker bars. Taking care of yourself physically often just isn't enough. Sometimes your house catches fire or you become sick or even disabled. This is where insurance comes in.

For the right price, you can insure just about anything, but why should you? Again, your insurance needs are based on your individual requirements. A man with young children and a stay-at-home wife needs more life insurance than an older man with a grown family and an attorney for a wife. On the other hand, our bodies wear out with age, and a good medical policy is probably more important to the older couple.

As John B. Kelly says, "The only difference between a poor old widow and a beautiful lady is properly planned wealth (life insurance). The difference between a terrified existence and peace of mind for a disabled worker is disability insurance coverage!"

The best approach to insurance is to assess your needs and shop around for the best package to fulfill those needs. Carefully consider the amount of risk you are willing to assume in determining a deductible and coverage and review your insurance requirements on a regular basis.

An important philosophy of life is to make the most of what you have. Learn to turn problems into opportunities. If you are handed a lemon — make lemonade.

The significance of money and possessions in today's society cannot be overlooked. The most satisified people are the ones who are able to distinquish the great difference between what they have and what they are.

By all means enjoy the fruits of your labor, but also start. saving for your future.

While not everybody can be financially wealthy, we can all be fulfilled by enjoying what we do have.

Chapter 6

Health — More Than Just Minding Body and Soul

Nothing contributes more to the quality of life than good health.

> **He who has health has hope; and he who has hope has everything.**
> **— Arabian Proverb**

It is most important that you take care of your physical body and your emotional well-being. You are provided with only one basic body, even though you may shed skin, lose hair and have other parts of your body mended or replaced during your lifetime.

When it comes to matters of health, moderation is the best policy in eating, drinking and exercise.

Let me quote from Art Linkletter on this subject:

"Any high quality of life that I enjoy has been based upon excellent health, given to me by unknown parents (I was adopted) and diligent caretaking of that good health. I have never smoked or drank, nor been physically out of shape. At age 80, I ski in the winter and surf in Hawaii in the summer."

Art Linkletter has certainly lived a full and enviable life and yet he has had a lot of emotional turmoils, including the loss of a daughter due to drug addiction.

A factor in the health of Art Linkletter, as is true of all of us, is genes. Although, you cannot select the genes you receive, you should be aware of how they affect your life.

Even though your biological parents may have had a tendency to be over or underweight, this does not mean you too are destined to be obese or unduly thin. However, genes do influence your physical health in many respects. Your life expectancy, to a large degree, can be predicted based upon the longevity of your parents and grandparents.

It is helpful to know the medical history of your parents so you may guard against illness and take preventative measures, if for example, there is heart disease, cancer or diabetes in the family.

The awareness of these factors and taking the appropriate steps may help extend your life, or make life more enjoyable. Sensible eating and wise living may not add 30 years to your life, but doing so may well add several years.

Quality of Life: Health

Arnold Fox, M.D., stated that in his 37 years of experience as an internist and cardiologist, he has found that people with higher incomes live longer and are healthier. "Pulling yourself up, as so many Americans have done, from poverty and lower socio-economic status not only helps your bank account but it is extremely helpful to your health."

An article in the October 1993 issue of the American Heart Association Journal, *Circulation*, describing a study conducted over the past 40 years supports Dr. Fox. "There was a striking relationship between lower socio-economic status (SES) and the increased risk of atherosclerosis, heart and blood vessel disease and premature death."

As Dr. Fox points out, "And it doesn't end with you. Children of lower SES, unless they pull themselves up, will continue to have increased mortality and morbidity — hardened blood vessel disease, stroke, and heart attack, while those of the upwardly mobile will have considerably less."

> **The only way to keep your health is to eat what you don't want, drink what you don't like, and do what you'd druther not.**
> **— Mark Twain**

Fortunately for us, Mr. Twain's observations on health aren't necessarily true.

One health issue of concern is weight control. Amazingly, one in every four Americans considers him or herself to be a dieter.

Many adults who are overweight fault the instructions received as a child such as, "Clean your plate . . .", and "Remember the poor starving children. . ." Bad habits formulated in childhood are difficult to change. Behavior modification in a formalized way may need to be undertaken to be able to adjust to an appropriate intake.

A significant array of nutritional programs are available to assist in behavior modification. These programs are sponsored by health groups and hospitals. Many are offered at no or very low cost and may even be covered by insurance.

There are a myriad of diets available to those wishing to eliminate excess weight. The successful ones have two things in common. First, the philosophy that you don't "go on" a diet (any diet you "go on" is one you will "go off"), but that you make a lifetime decision to choose healthier foods prepared in a healthier manner. Second, there is no magical formula, special food or miracle drug which will "melt those pounds away" while you sleep, work, or even eat anything you want.

If the number of calories consumed exceeds the number of calories used, the result will be a weight gain. Likewise, if calories used is more than calories consumed, weight loss will result.

To lengthen thy life, lessen thy meals.
— Benjamin Franklin

"Wow, you look great — you've lost a lot of weight!" I exclaimed to a friend I hadn't seen in several months. To which Gil Eagles replied, "I have no intention of 'finding' any weight I may have 'lost' — those pounds are G-O-N-E forever!"

Quality of Life: Health

> **Attribute my longevity to the fact that I use meat as a condiment...**
> — **Thomas Jefferson**

Dr. Arnold Fox, who wrote *Immune For Life* recommends a Super Food Diet which emphasizes a low fat, low cholesterol, high complex carbohydrate and moderate protein diet. Super foods include fruits and vegetables, whole grains, low fat fish, poultry, beans, lentils, nuts and seeds.

In addition to being better for you, the Super Foods can also be less expensive. Consider potatoes. The next time you're at the grocery store, compare the price of a pound of raw potatoes with the price of an 8 ounce bag of potato chips. While a plain cooked potato is low in fat (it's the butter, sour cream, bacon and cheese you put on it that racks up the fat and calories), potato chips are 64% fat!

Pure water is also a vital daily nutrient. It has no fat, cholesterol or calories. Our bodies are approximately 50-60% water and need continual replenishment. So be good to your body. Give it lots of water, not coffee, tea or soda, but pure water. Drink six to eight 8 ounce glasses of water each day. You can drink water with every meal, as well as other times throughout the day.

Of course, changing your diet alone has proven to be an ineffective way to maintain your weight. Exercise is also a vital part of any health maintenance program.

Are you a couch potato? Do you get all your exercise from looking for the channel changer?

Maintaining a good physical condition not only adds years to your life, but life to your years.

People who maintain a regular exercise program are motivated, feel better, live longer and are healthier.

Fortunately for you and me the "No Pain, No Gain" philosophy has been replaced by a more reasonable approach to exercise. There are a multitude of health clubs you can join offering everything from low-impact aerobics classes to body-building and weight-training as well as a wide variety of affordable exercise equipment you can purchase to create your own "home" gym. If you enjoy this type of activity and will make a commitment to follow a program, then by all means do so.

I've found the only exercise equipment I need is a good pair of walking shoes. A 15 to 20 minute spirited walk three or four times a week can do much to increase your energy level and reduce stress.

The sovereign invigorator of the body is exercise, and of all the exercises, walking is best.
— Thomas Jefferson

Quality of Life: Health

Drinking alcoholic beverages is generally all right when done in moderation. I say generally, because some people cannot tolerate alcohol in any quantity and must vigorously fight their addiction. You also need to be careful when taking prescription medicine — alcohol can often intensify or alter its effects.

My final word on alcohol relates to drinking and driving and that word is "DON'T." Not only is this a dangerous practice, (for you as well as other drivers on the road) but it's not worth the risk of being arrested, paying a high fine, and having your insurance premiums increased. If you are drinking away from home, be sure to have a designated driver or call a taxi.

You can eat right and drink right and still be poisoning your body. Our industrialized society has created a significant by-product — pollutants — which are in the land, air and water.

The coach of a junior high soccer team said, "I have inhalers in my pocket for four of the boys. When did so many kids start to get asthma?"

The good news is the pollution problem has been identified and laws are being enacted to control the causes of these problems.

I strongly encourage you to support *sensible* laws that clean up our environment. After all, if you can't breathe, what else is there?

Another pollution problem is much more personal and that is smoking. Medical experts now tell us the single best thing you can do to improve your health and life expectancy is to stop smoking.

New medical evidence of the harm caused by second-hand smoke is alarming. Tobacco smoke contains more than 4,000 chemicals and at least 40 known carcinogens. Studies have shown that early exposure in life to second hand smoke increases the chances of plaque development in the arteries. Certainly you can avoid being around someone who is smoking excessively so that second-hand smoke does not contaminate your body.

Many businesses and governments are stating that while they cannot totally prohibit people from smoking, they can require that it be done outdoors or in designated areas or only at designated times.

Another important aspect of personal health is safety. There are several things you can easily do to greatly increase your safety.

You might not think of automobile maintenance as part of your safety routine, but consider the consequences of a break-down. On a busy highway, you increase your chances of being struck by another car or if you are on a deserted back road, you may not be able to summon help. Worn tires can cause a blow out, resulting in your losing control of the car.

> Have your car serviced regularly by a trusted mechanic, learn how to check your oil and water levels, and fill your gas tank before it reaches the big "E".

How you drive can also have a big effect on your safety. Statistically, almost 90% of all automobile accidents occur within 10 miles of home. Phyllis Diller said that when her husband, Fang, heard this statistic he decided to move!

Quality of Life: Health

Sandy always wore her seat belt when out on the highway, but thought it was too much trouble around town. Then one day she went to pick up her children from school and passed the scene of an accident that had occurred just moments before. "It was awful. This woman had been thrown out of the car and was killed. Her car had been hit by a drunk driver while she was on her way to pick up her kids. She probably would have been all right if she had worn a seat belt. I realized then and there that you don't need to be on the highway to be involved in a fatal accident. Now, I buckle up every time I get in the car. I can't even drive across a parking lot without my seat belt fastened. And everyone riding with me buckles up, too. I tell them the car won't start unless all the seat belts are buckled."

In fact, many states have laws requiring that all passengers wear their seat belts any time the car is in use.

Break up long trips by planning rest stops every two or three hours. Get out of the car, stretch your legs, drink a cup of coffee, a glass of water or a soft drink. You may arrive at your destination a few minutes later, but you'll feel much better. One caveat though, because of the popularity of car-jackings, be sure to pick a well-lighted, highly populated area to stop.

Drive with the flow of traffic, not significantly faster or slower. To ease the stress of long trips, I listen to inspirational tapes or stories on cassette.

Always lock your car when driving. Electric door locks and windows used to be considered a luxury, but now I think of them as essential safety equipment.

Be aware of your surroundings. Out on the highway, know the traffic around you. In the city, don't accidentally wander into "no man's land." At night, park only in well-lit, populated areas, and have your keys ready when you reach your car. If you have concerns about your safety, ask a security officer to walk you to your car.

Don't get distracted from your main function — driving the car. Numerous highway patrol departments have noted the various things drivers were cited for doing while driving. Among them were reading the newspaper, shaving, putting on make-up, changing clothes and even changing a baby's diaper!

Safety in the home is often a matter of common sense.

By all means, install smoke alarms and change the batteries regularly. Marie keeps her smoke alarm batteries fresh by changing them whenever the time switches between standard and daylight savings.

Families with small children have usually child-proofed their homes. Dangerous chemicals, medicines and matches are locked away. However, households without small children may not have taken these precautions.

I picked up an interesting safety tip one day when I observed my assistant accidentally drop a pair of scissors. Instead of reaching to catch the scissors before they hit the floor, she jumped back from them. Sarah told me "I've made it a habit not to try to catch falling objects. The automatic reaction is to try to catch it, whether it's a knife, a hot pan or a dish. If you catch it,

you can cut or burn yourself. If you miss it, it can land on your feet and do damage. Yes, I've broken a few dishes I probably could have saved, but I think I've come out ahead with fewer cuts, bruises and broken toes."

> Another specific aspect of good health is quality sleep. Consistently obtaining adequate amounts of sleep is vital to maintaining a healthy body.

The National Commission on Sleep Disorders Research estimates that some 40 million Americans have sleep disorders and that millions more suffer from lack of sleep. One of the biggest myths about quality sleep is that everyone requires the same amount. Research now shows that individual sleep patterns vary widely from 4 1/2 to 10 hours of sleep required per night. 65% of the population is estimated to need anywhere from 6 1/2 to 8 1/2 hours of sleep.

Losing an hour or two of sleep here and there may not seem like an immediate problem and at first you probably won't even notice a difference. As your sleep deficit builds, this seemingly minor loss of sleep begins to take effect, hitting your brain long before your body shows signs of fatigue. Lack of sleep can adversely affect your concentration, memory and alertness, as well as lower your patience level.

> A higher quality of sleep results when you retire at a consistent hour and rise at about the same time every day.

Once you have determined the number of hours of sleep you need, be sure to maintain a regular sleep pattern as the body has trouble adjusting to changes in sleeping habits. Researchers now say if you must rely on an alarm clock to wake up every morning and if you sleep more than an hour or two longer on weekends than on weekdays, you are probably suffering from chronic sleep deprivation.

Other factors affect the quality of sleep each individual receives. Most people find a good mattress contributes to a more restful sleep. Some need their own personal pillow and may even carry it with them on trips.

While some people find it difficult to share a bed, others sleep poorly away from their loved one.

The temperature at night can have a major impact upon the body's ability to rejuvenate. Having a flow of fresh air is preferred to artificially cooled air and studies have found the ideal air temperature is under 70 degrees.

Many people have a preferred position for sleeping and if you are in a new place or a different environment where you cannot stretch out, move around or feel comfortable you may find your sleep patterns disrupted.

One doctor says, "Notice your position when you wake up. You may go to sleep every night lying on your back. But if you wake up on your right side, that means your body adjusted to the most comfortable and effective position for you. Try going to sleep on your right side. You will find you fall asleep sooner, and have a more restful night."

It is sometimes difficult to fall asleep. This often occurs when your mind is so concerned or preoccupied that you cannot release thoughts sufficiently to let the physical process of sleep take over. When that happens, many people find it worthwhile to get up, read, write, walk or do something relaxing and then return to bed.

In addition, drinking warm milk or eating bananas helps some people relax. Milk and bananas contain tryptophan, a natural sleep inducer.

Over reliance on sleeping pills can become counter-productive. Some of these products can leave you feeling groggy in the morning and others can cause short-term memory loss.

Reducing the intake of liquids, in particular alcohol and caffeine, a few hours before bedtime helps to improve the quality of sleep and rest. If you are sensitive to caffeine, keep in mind that the effects of caffeine can last for over 24 hours. One rule is to eat nothing after 6 p.m. and drink nothing after 8 p.m. if you want to establish 10 p.m. as your bedtime.

Naps are more beneficial if taken before 4 p.m. and for less than an hour (20 minutes is the recommended ideal). Otherwise, they begin to interfere with established sleep patterns.

I cannot overemphasize the value of periodic medical checkups as suggested by the AMA Guidelines, as well as, regular visits to your dentist and other health care providers. Regular examinations can often lead to early detection of problems that are not otherwise evident. Tests can reveal conditions such as high blood pressure or high cholesterol. These tests may give you several years of advance notice of a potential problem and allow adequate time for necessary treatment.

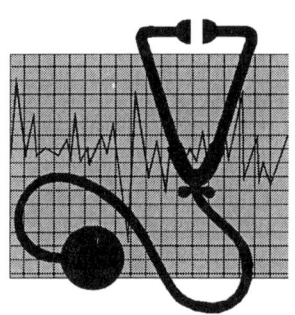

Listen to your body. Only patients have symptoms and while they can seek out a doctor's advice, symptoms belong only to the patient.

Remember, you, not your doctor, are responsible for your health care. If your doctor doesn't listen to you, find one that does. If you have a question about a procedure, ask. And if you're not satisfied with the answer, seek a second opinion. Doctors are highly trained professionals and we tend to regard them as infallible, but doctors can and do make mistakes.

Richard found this out the hard way when he broke his wrist. "The side of my wrist stuck way out, but the doctor said it was only swelling when he put a cast on my arm. It wasn't until

Quality of Life: Health

two weeks later that it was discovered that my bone was displaced and should have been set. It turned out that the angle of the X-ray didn't clearly show the displacement.

"I had to have my wrist re-broken and, of course, the healing period was extended. In addition, the wrist never healed correctly. I have to live with a slightly deformed wrist and some pain.

"My common sense told me, just by looking at it, that the bone needed to be set. I wish now I had insisted on a second opinion from an orthopedist. I could have saved myself a lot of pain and suffering."

Modern technology has made it possible to replace almost any part of the body, not just vital organs. We know it is possible to reattach an arm, finger or tooth. Other organs such as the heart and liver may be transplanted from a donor.

However, these previously owned body parts are never as good as healthy original ones. Transplant patients must continually take drugs to fight tissue rejection and sometimes have to endure a second transplant or additional operations.

Keeping your physical body in good shape and solid condition may pay big dividends when you least expect it. Periodically, we hear about people lost in the wilderness and able to survive because they were in good physical condition or able to walk a considerable distance to get out alive.

A body in good shape can withstand physical and mental stress much longer than one which is not.

Health issues refer to more than the physical body. Our emotional well being is critical to overall health. This takes more than just thinking positive thoughts.

When you are unable to sort out all the emotional turmoil in life, seeking the assistance of professionals is encouraged. More and more people are willing to admit they have been or are in therapy for problems which are a regular part of life's experiences.

With medical advances, many who in times past would have been deemed mentally ill and unfit to interact with society are today leading healthy and productive lives.

Support groups are very helpful because they allow people to see that there are others suffering from the same mental stresses or physical abuses. Support groups also offer an opportunity to openly discuss, without fear of judgement, ways to cope with everyday struggles.

People who are depressed, unhappy or simply not adjusting well in life can benefit from attending support groups. Many experience a change in attitude after they meet people and listen to the stories shared in these groups.

While therapists have been criticized, there is much to be said about having someone listen to you without judgement, without interruption and who is trained to pick up nuances that laymen cannot detect.

Others to whom you tell your troubles may be well-meaning and agreeable, but may use a lot of "shoulds" in responding to your comments.

Do not let others "should" on you. Qualified therapists seldom do so. They may offer observations and possible suggestions along with ideas, thoughts and insights.

> You need to do whatever you determine is
> appropriate for you, not necessarily what
> others have decided you "should" do.

Deepak Chopra, M.D. author of *Ageless Body, Timeless Mind*, recommends listening to your body's wisdom, which expresses itself through signals of comfort and discomfort. When choosing a certain behavior, ask your body, "How do you feel about this?" If your body sends a signal of physical or emotional distress, watch out. If your body sends a signal of comfort and eagerness, proceed.

Take time to be silent, to meditate, to quiet the internal dialogue. Pay attention to your inner life, so that you can be guided by intuition rather than what other people tell you is good or not good for you.

While it is comforting to know that professional help is available, many emotional problems are caused by plain old stress.

Stress management is a popular topic for seminars and magazine articles. Much of our stress is caused by frustration with daily living: The guy who cuts you off on the freeway; the boss

who expects the impossible; the lines at the post office; the Internal Revenue Service.

Following the hints on nutrition and exercise discussed earlier is your first defense against stress, as well as disease. Next is your sense of humor. You can be witty or corny, but laughing is a great stress reliever. The next time you are stuck in traffic, try blowing soap bubbles or putting on a funny nose. Isn't that more relaxing than tightening your grip on the steering wheel, honking the horn and giving the "international salute"?

Finally, try to "let it go." Don't dwell on problems over which you have no control. Don't let anger overwhelm your life.

You will experience emotional turmoil in your life. Some helps you grow and some seems to be nothing more than a burden. Dealing with stress is more of a re-orientation of the way you look at life. It is a change in perception more than a change in your style of managing the stressful experiences and events.

I am upset, not by events, but rather by the way I view them.
— **Epicetus**

Free expression of loving, positive emotions are essential components of a healthy life.

Age, like love, cannot be hidden.
— **William Shakespeare**

As we age, our focus on health changes. Young people tend to take their good health for granted. They can eat

Quality of Life: Health

wonderfully greasy french fries and not be up all night with indigestion; they can play volleyball over the weekend and not be ready for traction on Monday; they can stay up all night dancing or completing a term paper and actually function the next day.

> **Youth is wasted on the young.**
> **— George Bernard Shaw**

We become more and more concerned with conserving our health and lessening the demands we put on our bodies as we grow older. Activities don't need to cease when we are no longer gainfully employed. Perhaps it is only a change of pace.

"People keep asking me to retire," George Burns said. "They say you are supposed to slow down and take it easy when you get old. If I had started slowing down when I was 65 or 70, by now I'd be stopped. A turtle would move faster."

> **It is better to wear out than rust out.**
> **— Old Proverb**

"But I didn't slow down. I kept going, and now there isn't a turtle around that can pass me."

> **George Burns had another quip when someone asked him, "When are you going to retire?" and he replied, "To what?"**

The overall benefit of a balanced lifestyle was highlighted by a population study conducted by UCLA researchers from 1965 to 1971. The study showed that as people with good habits moved

through life they could expect to enjoy an advantage in health over those who had bad habits. Thirty years later, no one has challenged this major conclusion: a balanced lifestyle is one of the more important steps towards retarding the aging process.

> **Take care of yourself. Good health is everyone's major source of wealth. Without it, happiness is almost impossible.**
> **— Lloyd Shearer**

Your quality of life is based upon the quality of your decisions and the quality of your intentions. Living a quality, fulfilling life is maximized with vibrant health. Your health can positively or negatively affect all the other areas of your life.

Chapter 7

Leisure — Avoid the Syndrome of All Work & No Play

What do you like to do when you're not working? How do you fill your leisure hours? Do you *have* any leisure hours? What activities do you find relaxing?

The concept of leisure is one of diversion from your regular work activities. Something that is relaxing, a change of pace, a reprieve from the stresses of your normal routine is the very essence of leisure.

> Some of us get so busy making a living that we forget to make a life.

How you choose to rest and relax depends on a number of factors including personality, health, age, gender and career choice.

One modern philosopher says, "There are two ways to take a vacation or break from work. One is to do something strenuous or busy, but different. The other way is to relax, lay around, watch the world go by and just do nothing."

In days past, social activities often revolved around accomplishing projects — quilting bees, barn raising, corn husking parties and so on.

I fondly remember as a child, accompanying my Grandmother to her women's church groups where she and the other women socialized while they made quilts and knitted sweaters for the less fortunate.

As social commentator Marshall McLuhan has observed, when an activity ceases to be a necessary part of our lives, it often turns into a hobby. Examples of this phenomenon are needle crafts, wood working, gardening, and to some extent, gourmet cooking.

> Physically active people working in offices are more likely to choose vigorous exercise than those who spend their work days caring for children or mowing lawns.

Professional speaker Mark Sanborn notes that one big benefit he receives from his adventures (trips to Borneo and Galapagos, river rafting, etc.) is that they offer

Quality of Life: Leisure

a complete change of pace or shift of context. "Some of my best thinking and creating is done during an adventure. It's a 'mental jolt.' Also, adventure brings the priorities of life into focus."

> It is important to find leisure activities you enjoy.
> Ones you find fulfilling as well as relaxing;
> stimulating as well as pleasurable.

As our lives become more complex and the pressures of career and family overwhelm us, "A lot of us are 'vegging out' — becoming couch potatoes — which can be more numbing than renewing," notes futurist Roger Selbert, Ph.D. "The most popular forms of leisure today are television watching and resting."

Television's popularity can be attributed to the lack of effort required to participate, once the remote control has been located.

> Hopefully, you will develop a variety of interests.
> You need pursuits that allow you quiet and solitude
> to explore your inner-self; you will want hobbies
> you can share with family and friends; you will
> want diversions that are relaxing; and you will want
> activities that require physical exertion to relieve
> stress and improve health.

Surveys are forecasting shopping for fun, traveling, walking for exercise, camping, hiking, skiing, home improvement and gardening as the popular activities for the '90s.

Surprisingly, taking time for leisure activities is taking responsibility for yourself. Without the chance for recreation, you become stale and tired. Think of "recreation" as the opportunity to "re-create" yourself on a regular basis.

It is interesting that we use the expression "play ball," but not "work ball." You should have activities you look forward to and think of as truly play and not necessarily as work. What is play for one is work for another and vice versa. It all depends on your point of view and attitude.

A second grade teacher was showing pictures of people engaged in various activities to her students. One of the pictures showed two men. One man was sitting in a chair, reading a book; the other man was weeding a garden. "Janey, which man is working and which man is having fun?" asked Miss Carr. And Janey replied, "The man with the book is working and the man with the hoe is having fun!" Of course, Miss Carr was rather surprised at this answer and asked Janey to explain further. "My Daddy's a doctor, he reads a lot of books and magazines for his job. When he wants to relax he works in the garden."

Then there are people like Dwayne who are lucky enough to work at their hobby. Dwayne's passion is computers. Says his wife, Dorothy, "Yes, it's true, I am a computer widow. Dwayne turns the computer on as soon as he gets up to check for messages on computer bulletin boards. Then he goes to work where he spends his day working with and on computers. He's the unofficial computer expert for his department. Co-workers always go to him first with problems. At night, he plays computer games with our son and does computer drafting for a second income.

Quality of Life: Leisure

He's on that thing so much, I have to fight to get my turn with the computer, but at least I always know where to find him."

Obviously Dwayne derives a lot of satisfaction from the computer. Others extend their regular jobs into their leisure activities as well, such as the baseball player who coaches Little League, the auto repairman who is restoring a Model-T with his son, and the taxi driver who likes to take his family on long drives.

Many people find sports to be an ideal pastime.

Remember you don't have to play like a pro to have a good time. Although you will probably have a better time playing with others at your skill level, you may learn more and improve faster by playing with those who are better than you.

Some sports require active team participation, such as baseball or soccer; while other sports such as handball or bicycling can be more of a solo activity.

A sport like handball provides a physical opportunity to relieve frustrations. Instead of kicking the dog, you can hammer away at the ball.

At other times, you may choose the role of spectator. Mel had been a dyed-in-the-wool Dodgers baseball fan for forty years. He knew all the statistics and was always involved. When the Los Angeles Dodgers were playing, if he couldn't be at the game, he was plugged into a radio or in front of the television set. His greatest thrill would have been to participate in a "Fantasy Sports Camp" where he could go to Spring training with the Dodgers.

In high school Mel had been an outstanding ball player, had gone to college on a sports scholarship and entertained the notion of becoming a professional baseball player.

Unfortunately, a serious motorcycle accident ended his active participation in baseball. But, by changing the focus of his involvement from participant to observer, he still enjoys his favorite sport.

Some people can take up an enjoyable hobby with little pre-investment of money or time and then there are those like Bill.

Bill is a "Type A" personality who decided to take up photography. "Being me, I figured I had to go whole hog. I bought the camera with the most bells and whistles I could find. And attachments — boy, did I have attachments — lenses, tripod, carrying case to keep it all together. I signed up for photography lessons at our community college. Of course within a month, I just had to have a dark room, so I converted some unused space in my house.

"After all this time and money investment, I took about a dozen rolls of pictures before I lost interest in the whole thing."

Bill told me this story while we were having coffee in his home. I looked around and commented on the framed photos of his children.

Quality of Life: Leisure

"Oh those," he said sheepishly. "Those were taken by my wife with her little point-and-shoot camera and developed at the corner drug store."

Bill became so involved in the accoutrements of his hobby, he forgot to find out if it was something he would enjoy. As Bill's story also illustrates, it's not necessary to have the newest, most expensive equipment to receive pleasure from a pastime.

I suspect part of Bill's problem was all the fuss and bother that accompanied the picture-taking process. By the time he had unpacked all of the equipment and set up the camera, he had become bored. On the other hand, his wife enjoyed taking simple, but quality pictures with her inexpensive camera.

Rita and Tom enjoy watching movies. The only problem is Rita likes "soupy love stories and silly musicals" (Tom's description) while Tom only wants to see "car chases, blood and guts and really stupid comedies" (Rita's description). While there was an occasional movie upon which they both agreed, they each felt deprived of their favorites.

"Tom finally hit on the solution," Rita told me. "We go to the multi-screen theater. Tom sees his movie and I see mine. Afterwards we talk and share the plots over a snack together."

Others find traveling to be an interesting way to fill their leisure hours.

Steffie and Greg work hard all year to save enough money to take a really grand three week vacation each summer. "All our energies were geared towards these wonderful vacations. One summer we packed up the kids and drove through the Western

states. Another time we flew to Europe and visited probably a thousand museums and cathedrals.

"You can't imagine how much pressure we put on ourselves to have a good time. On the European trip, just about everything that could go wrong did. They lost our reservations in Paris, the kids drank the water in one country and we managed to arrive in another city just after terrorists had blown up the airport. We just tried to do and see everything Europe had to offer. It became one of those, 'If this Is Tuesday, It Must Be Belgium' kind of vacations.

"Needless to say, we came home exhausted, frustrated and broke."

Steffie went on to say she and Greg had some serious discussions about what they wanted out of a vacation.

"We came to realize that we needed something more relaxing. Now we take several mini-vacations throughout the year. Long weekends with no special plans — just laze about in the sunshine, read, talk. Sometimes we take the kids, sometimes we leave them at Grandma's.

"We still want to travel, but it's going to be at a slower pace, without unrealistic expectations."

Ginger and Justin are another couple who believe in mini-vacations. "We used to plan for a leisurely long weekend at home, but it never worked out that way," Justin told me.

"There was always some job around the house that needed doing, or people would call who didn't understand our need to be alone. We finally found that we could really get some 'R and R' by checking into a hotel. Sometimes we didn't even leave town, but just that little change in scenery — getting away even just a couple of miles, was enough to let us recharge our batteries."

Others find they can manage to fit rest and relaxation into even the busiest schedules.

Marge is a wife and mother of three who spends her workdays as a teller in a busy bank. "I used to get home, exhausted from being on my feet all day, and the first thing anyone said to me was 'What's for dinner?' Trying to get dinner on the table became a real chore. I was always yelling at the kids and fighting with my husband."

Fortunately Marge realized that she needed some quiet time to herself after her work day. " I sat everyone down and together we came up with a great plan. Before I get home, the kids put together a snack for all of us. It might be popcorn, granola bars, sliced veggies and dip or a small salad. That takes the edge off everybody's hunger. Then when I get home, I get a half an hour all to myself. As long as everybody's breathing and nobody's bleeding, I'm not to be disturbed. I usually spend that time reading or soaking in the tub – just unwinding. When my half hour's up, I'm ready to interact with my family. Now everybody helps with dinner – it's become a fun family activity that I really enjoy."

> **You will never *find* time for anything. If you want time, you must *make* it.**
> — Charles Burton

Many of us don't have the time we want or need to devote to leisure activities because we haven't learned to manage our time effectively. With so many demands on our time, we find leisure is stuffed into our spare time and we have no time to spare. In 1993, independent researchers noted that 48% of Americans feel as though they have less leisure time than they did five years ago.

Researcher John Robinson, a sociology professor at University of Maryland has found that Americans actually have more time available for leisure activities than they think, but with so much to choose from, even unwinding has become work. Life in the '90s offers more choices than there are hours in the day.

Robinson believes this to be the paradox of the '90s lifestyle. "The pace of life is so fast that even a leisure activity like watching TV is more stressful than it used to be. There are so many ways we can spend our free time, even the decision to do nothing causes a lot of stress."

> **Take control of your time, or time will control you.**
> — Vince Bartolone

There are a few techniques I would like to pass along to you to enable you to make more of your time.

Quality of Life: Leisure

If you are one of those people who constantly works hard yet never seems to get anything accomplished, you need to learn to focus on goals instead of activities. So often we perform out of habit without considering whether the activity is productive or even necessary. Therefore, think about what you do and why you do it.

Get organized! Eric was a junior executive with little chance of becoming a senior executive because of the constant disarray of his office. "I'd been told that my people skills were excellent and my technical abilities outstanding, but I could never seem to find what I needed. Once something hit my desk, it seemed to enter the Bermuda Triangle, never to be seen again. I almost lost my job when an important contract wasn't completed on time. My supervisor made it very clear to me that my career would not advance until I became organized.

"After reading some literature on organization, I realized my problem was a lack of decisiveness. Papers would appear in my basket, I would read them, and then could never decide what to do with them. A notification of a seminar? Better hold on to that — might want to go, might not. Professional journals? There's an article in this issue I should read, better throw it into my briefcase. Of course, my briefcase was already full of magazines with articles I really should read. I got all my exercise just lugging that briefcase around. Letter from a client? I ought to respond to it before I file it, but before I respond, I need to ... Well, you get the picture.

"I learned I need to process papers, not shuffle them. I either needed to schedule the seminar if I was going or throw away the notice. It took awhile, but eventually I did get organized and I did become a senior executive!"

Learn to delegate. Even people without employees can and do delegate. Think about it. Do you raise lambs in the back yard, shear their wool, comb it, spin it, weave it into cloth, cut out and sew your own clothes?

The one or two who say yes probably don't also drill their own oil wells, pump and refine the oil to put gas in their cars.

We all rely on others to perform services for us. Sometimes we can make the best use of our time by hiring more services.

All of us have chores we enjoy, chores we tolerate and chores where we'd rather have a root canal — minus the Novocaine. The root canal type chores are the ones you should, if possible, hire someone else to do.

Julie and Brandy have worked out an arrangement whereby they have delegated their least favorite chore and it hasn't cost them a penny.

Julie hates ironing almost as much as she likes having neatly pressed clothes. On the other hand, Brandy doesn't mind ironing but she balances her checkbook by changing banks. Her phone and electricity are turned off at least twice a year because she doesn't make the payments on time. Twice a month Julie and Brandy get together. Brandy does all Julie's ironing and Julie writes all the checks for Brandy's bills, reconciles her bank statement and keeps all the tax information together.

Quality of Life: Leisure 147

Mothers with outside jobs never seem to have enough leisure time between juggling work and home responsibilities. These women can delegate to their children. Even children as young as three can help set or clear the table, pick up their own room and empty trash cans.

Older children can do their own laundry. They'll probably turn their underwear pink only once before they learn not to wash a red sweatshirt with the white stuff.

Explain to your children the concept of "no free lunch." It will help you out and builds character in them.

Make "To Do" lists and prioritize them. Get that feeling of satisfaction when you check off jobs you've completed. This is a good technique for determining which job needs to be completed first.

Monitor your performance level. If you work better in the morning, try to reserve those hours to put uninterrupted time into preparing that contract or report.

Stop being a perfectionist. You should strive for excellence, but if you don't complete a job until it is perfect, you'll never complete it. Perfectionists also have a hard time delegating. Since nobody can do the job as well as they can, they try to do their job and everybody elses, too.

Learn to say, "No." We've all heard the saying, "If you want something done, ask a busy person." If you are that busy person and you don't want to do it — just say no! (Don't try this

with your boss or you may end up with more leisure time than you bargained for!)

> All of us are often asked to give of our time for various worthy causes. By all means, contribute to the causes you believe in and want to support. However, remember that your health and peace of mind are also a worthy cause. You can cut yourself up into so many little pieces that you end up not being helpful to anyone, including yourself.

Finally, stop procrastinating. Do It Now! Do the unpleasant task first; get it out of the way so you can work on the more pleasant things in your day. Break down large projects into smaller, doable sections.

One of the more unique aspects of leisure is the ability to combine your leisure activities with the other factors contributing to a balanced life.

Gene had attended one of my Quality of Life seminars. He called me up one day and said in an excited voice, "Dr. Jones, I finally did it!"

"Did what, Gene?" I asked.

"I finally managed to do one activity which covered all eight spokes of the wheel!"

As you can imagine, this piqued my curiosity. "And how did you manage to do this, Gene?"

Quality of Life: Leisure

"Well, my company (career) sponsored me in a Walk-A-Thon (health) for a local charity (community). I asked my wife to join me for companionship (family). She's a financial planner, you know, and during the course of the walk she informed me (education) about some new investment opportunities she thought we should take advantage of (financial). Of course, I enjoyed spending time with my wife during this event (leisure). The walk was quite a bit longer than I am accustomed to, but people were counting on me and I really felt as though some inner strength was sustaining me (spirituality)."

While I congratulated Gene on his achievement, you don't need to try to kill all eight birds with one stone every time. However, leisure does combine well with other factors.

> Sharing leisure activities with family and friends can be a lot of fun. Playing Monopoly with the kids, enjoying spectator sports with friends, taking long romantic walks with your loved one are all excellent ways to build relationships and special memories.

"I developed my enjoyment for games through playing with my grandfather," says Joan. "From the time I was a little girl, we would play together and I enjoyed my fair share of wins. Grandpa would start the game by handicapping himself. For instance, if we were playing checkers, he started out with fewer playing pieces. Then he would play as well as he could against me. As I improved, his handicap lessened until finally he no longer needed the handicap. I thought it was a wonderful system. I learned to be a good winner as well as a good loser. And I have wonderful memories of our time together."

In the community section, we discussed volunteer work and political involvement. If these activities provide a change of pace from your work day and are relaxing to you, they also fall under the leisure category.

Of course, health and exercise go hand in hand. Exercise is a great stress reliever as well as an excellent leisure activity for the athletically inclined.

The eight factors for a quality life are not independent of each other. They should be woven together to provide a rich fulfilling life.

**What we do during our working hours
determines what we have;
what we do during our leisure hours
determines what we are.**
— **George Eastman**

Chapter 8

Spirituality — Getting In Touch With Your Greater Self

Spirituality is a very personal sense of belief, usually dating back to childhood and the early beginnings of life. Spirituality refers to the belief in God, a higher power or a supreme being and the practice of ethical concepts. It is not necessarily the same as religion.

During times of stress, catastrophe or traumatic events, many people acknowledge turning to prayer, even though they had not previously considered themselves believers. Perhaps this has occurred to you at some point in your life. This may be considered an admission that there are helpful forces that cannot be defined specifically in terms of "things" or people.

In a humorous vein, here is a story of a man who was down on his luck — absolutely at the end of his rope. With no hope, no money, no job and no possibilities, he turned to God.

He said, "God, give me a sign. Any sign and I will consecrate my life to you — a life of absolute dedication for as long as I live."

At that instant he heard a knock at the door. He opened the door and there stood a lawyer who presented him with a check for $4.5 million as his inheritance from a previously unknown relative. He signed the lawyer's forms, the lawyer shook his hand in congratulations and left.

The man closed the door, looked up and said, "Never mind God, I've got it handled myself."

> **Every major religion of the world has similar ideas of love, the same goal of benefiting humanity through spiritual practice, and the same effect of making their followers into better human beings.**
> **— The Dalai Lama**

Spiritual people can be identified by their adherence to ethical principles such as the Ten Commandments and the Golden Rule. These concepts are very relevant to spirituality.

> **Do unto others as they want to be done unto.**
> **— The Platinum Rule**

Quality of Life: Spirituality

> **Do unto others as you would have them do unto you.**
> — The Golden Rule

> **Do not do unto others what you would not have them do unto you.**
> — The Silver Rule

> **What I do not wish others to do unto me, I also wish not to do unto others.**
> — Tauan-mu Tz'u,
> a student of Confucius

> **Repay kindness with kindness, but evil with justice.**
> — Confucius

Isn't it interesting to see how this simplest but most powerful principle is paraphrased so many times in so many different ways?

> To be most effective in our caring for others we best care for them as they want to be cared for. For example, when some people are feeling ill, they want to be left alone, whereas others want to be nurtured and pampered.

> **Practicing the Golden Rule is not a sacrifice; it is an investment.**
> — Author Unknown

Worship takes many forms, in many places, and in many ways. We think of traditional worship as attending a religious service in a house of worship on holy days. In addition many people faithfully tune to radio or television programs to receive inspiration and guidance.

There are those who prefer silent meditation by themselves in a remote place. Others experience spirituality and religion when they are in the midst of a crowd, such as at a revival meeting, where they become totally consumed or charged with the spirit.

Dr. Robert Schuller, creator of The Crystal Cathedral, took over a drive-in movie theater. He encouraged people to come in their cars, even if they were casually dressed, to participate in the worship services. Their participation was far more important than their outer attire. Dr. Schuller knows garments do not define spirituality. It is what's inside that counts.

Religion's in the heart, not in the knees.
— Douglas W. Jerrold

Some attending formal worship may not be all that spiritual, by the same token, many who are not in attendance are indeed very spiritual. Their thoughts and actions speak much clearer than attendance at religious services.

Just as our physical growth differs from person to person, so too does our spirituality grow in stages. E. Fowler, J. Piaget, E. Erikson and Kohlberg all have developed stage theories. M. Scott Peck, M.D. in his book, *Further Along the Road Less Traveled* defines four stages of spiritual growth.

Quality of Life: Spirituality

Stage One is "chaotic/antisocial." The people in this stage are completely unprincipled. While some may be capable of pretending to love others, all their relationships are actually self-serving and manipulative. As can be expected, those in Stage One are often in trouble and can be found in jails or hospitals. However, a Stage One person with self-discipline and ambition can obtain a position of power and even become President or a famous preacher.

People in Stage One frequently move to Stage Two through a sudden dramatic event.

Stage Two is "formal/institutional." Those in this stage are dependent on an institution to govern their actions. This institution can be prison, the military, a highly organized business or a religious affiliation. Stage Two church goers are very attached to the rituals of their religion. They tend to see God as an external punitive force watching their every move.

Peck calls Stage Three "skeptic/individual." Stage Three people have absorbed the principles of the church in Stage Two and have now begun to question the myths and superstitions embodied in church ritual. These people tend to be "truth seekers." They live ethical lives and are generally spiritually ahead of Stage Two people, but are not seen as being religious.

Stage Four is "mystical/communal." These people, in seeking the truth, have seen that many of the myths and superstitions of Stage Two are the truth. While Stage Two people want to see everything in black and white, Stage Four people accept the mystery of the world.

As Peck writes, "Indeed, one of the things that characterize all the world's great religions is that they seem to have the capacity to speak to people in both Stage Two and Stage Four as if the very teachings of a given religion have two different translations. To take an example from Judaism, Psalm 111 ends with 'The fear of the Lord is the beginning of wisdom.' At Stage Two this is translated to mean, 'When you start fearing that big cop in the sky, you really wise up.' That's true. At Stage Four it is translated to mean, 'The awe of God shows you the way to enlightenment.' And that's also true."

Peck makes it clear that not everyone falls into one of these four stages, that some are in all four stages and that movement between the stages is possible.

Peck's books, *The Road Less Traveled* and *Further Along the Road Less Traveled* are useful for anyone looking for guidance in exploring their spirituality.

There are several other authors whose works I have found to be inspirational.

Dr. Norman Vincent Peale published *The Power of Positive Thinking* in 1952. This book, which ranks close to the Bible as one of the all time best-sellers, espouses the philosophy of people helping themselves through prayer and positive thinking.

In addition to building The Crystal Cathedral, Dr. Robert Schuller has also written many books which I feel are helpful. My personal favorite is *The Be (Happy) Attitudes*.

Quality of Life: Spirituality

The spiritual writer nearest to my heart is the man after whom I was named, Dr. E. Stanley Jones. My parents had heard him speak prior to my birth and decided if they had a son, he would be named after this great Christian author and Methodist missionary to India.

Dr. E. Stanley Jones was an evangelist, a Christian statesman, and an advocate of God. His ability to help people reconcile their differences and his quest for peaceful resolution, earned him several nominations for the Nobel Peace Prize.

Dr. Jones preached approximately 60,000 sermons, probably more than any other man in history. In spite of his seriousness, he was also a jovial man. He liked to joke and stated on the occasion of his 88th birthday. "Life is fun at 88 — and getting funnier all the time!"

During the course of his life, Dr. Jones authored 28 books. While I have not been able to confirm this, a friend told me a story attributed to Dr. Jones. It seems as if someone was marvelling at how Dr. Jones was able to do and accomplish many things. He was asked, "When in the world do you ever find time to write being you are such an involved and busy person?" Dr. Jones replied, "Tuesday." The questioner then asked, "What do you mean 'Tuesday'?" His response was "Every Tuesday, I write. You see it is a matter of a commitment and a decision to do something rather than just think about it. Every Tuesday I write."

Bishop James K. Mathews, his son-in-law, knew Dr. Jones from 1939 until his death in 1973. He says this about Dr. Jones'

writing practices, "He was highly disciplined and used every spare moment for writing, usually early in the morning."

In his book, *Victorious Living*, published in 1936, Dr. Jones addressed primary questions, such as, "Is life a bubble or an egg?" Is there nothingness at the heart of our existence or is it filled with potential? In *Is the Kingdom of God Realism*, he analyzed whether things spiritual were unrealistic and idealistic — very nice but irrelevant to practical living. One of his best known books, *Abundant Living*, discussed the capability of earning a living without the ability to truly live.

Dr. Jones and Mahatma Ghandi were intimate friends and they corresponded for many years. Dr. Jones' fifteenth book, written in 1948, entitled *Mahatma Ghandi*, is about this man who showed "more of the spirit of Christ than perhaps any other man in East or West," by demonstrating to the world the power of non-violent cooperation. Ghandi was a political and spiritual leader of India who advocated non-violent civil disobedience.

It was Dr. Jones' book on Ghandi which convinced Dr. Martin Luther King, Jr. to adopt nonviolence in his fight for civil rights in the United States.

Dr. King is another man of great spirituality who dedicated his life to securing a better life for others.

Troubles are often the tools by which God fashions us for better things.
— Henry Ward Beecher

Quality of Life: Spirituality

We also think of Mother Teresa, who dedicated her life to serving the poorest of the poor, and Father Damien, who sacrificed his life for the lepers in Molokai, Hawaii.

Of course, not all self-sacrificing people are as well known.

Francis Hernandez is a young woman with a rough past. During her teens she was heavily involved with drugs. She had her first child at a very early age and seven children before she turned 24. However, Francis was finally able to break away from the drug-addicted father of her first five children and turned her life around.

After kicking the drug habit and staying clean for a year, she met Joe. They married and began making plans for the future. Unfortunately, during her seventh pregnancy, Francis was diagnosed with HIV — the viral predecessor to AIDS.

"I found out I was infected after I had been sober for three years and happily married for two. I was finally getting my life together, dreaming of buying a house, being a responsible person. But then my past caught up with me. And I can't escape it.

"I wish I could change what I did then, because I'm paying for it now in a way no one deserves. I don't want to die."

Francis didn't crawl into bed and wait to die. With other concerned women, she formed a group called Fighting AIDS Through Education — FATE. Through FATE, Francis speaks to groups of teenagers most at risk of contracting the AIDS virus. Her giving during the last few years of her short life is sure to save the lives of others.

Others can be giving without the threat of a death sentence.

Chuck Wall, Ph.D., a professor at Bakersfield College in California has led his class in a campaign to commit "Random Acts of Senseless Kindness." What a wonderful idea! This campaign has attracted world-wide attention and made the front page of over 150 newspapers in the United States alone.

Can you imagine the ripple effect of committing these random acts of senseless kindness?

As an example of these random acts, let me share with you the story of Sharon Brothers. Sharon is a former flight attendant, runway and print fashion model and licensed cosmetologist who volunteers her time to hold after-school beauty classes for disadvantaged junior high schoolers. While some would scoff and say that the last thing these children need is a course in how to wear makeup, Sharon's classes are much more than skin deep. Her classes emphasize poise, beauty and self-esteem through social skills. "I grew up in a Christian home with a mother who took time to teach us manners and to love other people regardless of their race or status. My mother stressed doing the right thing, which gave me a heart for people."

Sharon Brothers' work in building self-esteem is going to make a difference in the lives of those young girls.

> **If you give a man a fish, you can feed him for a day, but if you teach him to fish, you can feed him for a lifetime.**

Quality of Life: Spirituality

There are a myriad of programs and organizations aimed at giving a hand, not a hand out.

If you build with wood, it will rot.
If you build with stone, it will chip away.
If you build with steel, it will rust.
But if you build with human beings,
you build for eternity.
— Carl Stevens

Intergenerational programs such as AgeLink in North Carolina team up senior citizens with latch-key children for the benefit of all.

Adult literacy programs help adults acquire the reading skills needed to make a better life for themselves.

Alcoholics Anonymous (AA) is an organization founded in 1935 to help alcoholics overcome their addiction to alcohol.

AA defines alcoholism as a disease as well as a spiritual problem and seeks to control the problem through a twelve step program. The program teaches the alcoholic to recognize that he or she is powerless over alcohol and must seek help from a higher power.

Other organizations such as Overeaters Anonymous and Gamblers Anonymous have adopted the twelve step program for recovery.

When Al Wooten Jr. was murdered, his mother, Myrtle Faye Rumph, convinced the shooting was a result of random gang activity, decided to do something to help keep children out of gangs. She started a small after-school learning center in South Central Los Angeles to offer supplemental courses in everything from spelling to "learning to learn." This is an excellent example of helping others to help themselves.

To err is human, to forgive, divine.
— **Alexander Pope**

Others have become paralyzed by the hate they have experienced towards those who have harmed them.

Hatred is a luxury no one can afford.
— **Author Unknown**

Sherry was badly injured when a drunk driver ran a red light and broadsided her car. "My life was instantly changed by the negligent actions of another. Both of my legs were badly broken, and at first, we didn't know whether I would ever walk again. I was so full of hate against the person who hit me, I couldn't concentrate on what was really important — getting well.

"Whenever I had visitors, all I talked about was this awful person and the horrible thing he had done to me. Finally, my doctor told me I wasn't making the progress I should and if I was going to get well, I needed to concentrate *all* my efforts in that direction.

"He arranged for a counselor to see me, and with her help, I began to understand that my hate was hurting me as much as the

drunk driver had. She helped me get beyond my hate by forgiving the man who had hit me.

"It was one of the hardest things I've ever done, but once I was able to forgive, I began to heal — both physically and emotionally."

Today, Sherry walks with the help of a cane and works with the local chapter of Mothers Against Drunk Driving (M.A.D.D.).

> No matter your personal feelings on the outcome of the Rodney King trial, can any of us forget his impassioned pleas during the Los Angeles riots, "Can't we all just get along?"

And who can forget the forgiveness by Reginald Denny of the men who so brutally attacked him during those riots?

> Holding on to hate and other negative feelings stunts your spiritual growth. Hate can't hurt the person at which it's directed—hate can only hurt the hater.

> **I've had a few arguments with people, but I never carry a grudge. You know why? While you're carrying a grudge, they're out dancing.**
> **— Buddy Hackett**

Quality of Life: Spirituality

An anonymous writer once described the three keys to "Personal Power," to enhance love and manifest power throughout the world.

The first key is *Compassion*. This is the key you use to understand others. Compassion means you allow yourself to become the other person, by listening. If you are thinking about what is being said, you cannot be listening. Bear in mind that compassion does not mean that you must support or agree with all points of view. Compassion allows you to experience another person from his or her perspective.

The second key is *Humility*. Humility does not mean any sort of debasement or subservience. Humility refers to being respectful, without vanity or arrogance.

The third key is the result of the first two and is *Confidence*. Using your confidence with responsibility, translates into real personal power in the world.

When you express confidence without humility, your confidence will not know what it is confident of; not trusting in its self-direction, for it will have no foundation.

On the other hand, when you express confidence without compassion, you fail to acknowledge the integrity of others. Your confidence will appear to be aggressive and bombastic.

Quality of Life: Spirituality

If you apply both compassion and humility simultaneously, the confidence you express allows you to manifest true power in the world.

Whatever words you use, make them words which you speak freely and openly. However, your actions speak louder than your words. Let your actions so shine that all who know and see you recognize you as a truly spiritual person.

Feelings of spirituality may be worn on the cuff for all to see. Nevertheless, the more significant feelings are within the individual, displayed at appropriate times in relevant ways through sharing and giving.

It is far more important "to be a sermon" than "to preach a sermon."

Let your spirituality be contagious. Live and love your life so that others may love and appreciate you.

Conscience is God's presence in man.
— Emanuel Swedenborg

Integrate your spiritual self with its higher ideals and ethical behavior into your everyday life. As the Disney character Jiminy Cricket was fond of noting, "Let your conscience be your guide."

Lukewarmness I account a sin
As great in love, as in religion.
— Abraham Cowley

The key to fulfilling your personal spiritual life is to make time for prayer, meditation, religious service attendance, study, fellowship, or whatever actions your belief system supports.

Just as you would not ignore your career, your family, or your hobbies, you cannot ignore your spiritual life. Spirituality needs to be nurtured. It is not just something you can pick up when you need it and then let it fall back to the wayside. It should be a constant part of your life, exemplified by both your actions and your beliefs.

As a journeyer in life, you need to care for your spiritual health just as you would your physical and mental well-being.

The whole theory of the universe is directed unerringly to one single individual — namely to You.
— **Walt Whitman**

Conclusion

Now, what are *you* going to do to enhance the quality of *your* life?

In the Introduction, I asked you to score yourself on a scale of 1 to 10 to determine where you would place yourself as to self-satisfaction and happiness on the spokes of your wheel of life.

Draw 8 lines intersecting at the center to form the spokes of a wheel. Label each of these lines for the 8 factors discussed — *Family, Community, Education, Career, Finances, Health, Leisure, Spirituality* — plot your scores for each of the factors on the appropriate line. When you connect the dots, do you have a concentric circle or do you have one or two spokes greatly protruding beyond the others?

How smooth is the journey you are experiencing day by day as you travel down life's path? If it feels like the road is under construction (or the potholes need filling), are you really enjoying the trip?

You have a choice. You can continue to do as you have always been doing and you will continue to get what you have always been getting. But I suspect that what you really want is something more, something richer, something better.

If you didn't have the desire for a higher quality life, you would not have made the effort to read this book. Now you need to decide to realign and fine tune your personal internal mechanisms and change your life.

Treat your family like the precious jewels they are. If you are estranged from your family or friends, heal the wounds. Rejoice in the reconciliation.

Make a better quality life for everyone by becoming more involved in your community either through volunteer work or political activities. Reach out to others. You may be surprised to find them reaching back to you.

Continue to pursue your education. Don't ever stop learning. Be open and accepting of new and different ideas. Let the universe be your university.

Find the challenge in your career. Treat your job as more than just the place you go to every day in exchange for money. Learn to turn problems into opportunities.

Spend your hard-earned money wisely and save for the future. Poor decisions made now can limit the options available to you later. Measure the amount of risk your are willing to accept in your investments by how comfortable you feel about them. Have faith in yourself!

Quality of Life: Conclusion

Take care of your physical body and mental state of mind. Eat plenty of good, healthy food, get adequate exercise and sleep peacefully. Good health is the most basic contribution to a quality life.

Learn to manage time better so that you can participate in leisure activities. Whether it's skiing down a mountain, playing ball with your kids or reading the latest best-seller, you need time to re-create yourself on a regular basis.

And, don't forget to explore your spiritual life. There are many fine examples of others whose lives are an inspiration to us all. Cast away from hate and embrace forgiveness and love.

But most importantly, follow your dreams. In looking back over your life will you say "I wish I had . . ." or will you proudly exclaim, "I'm glad I did . . . !"?

Even doing nothing and accepting the status quo doesn't mean changes won't happen in your life. The only thing constant about life is that it's always changing. And the rate of change seems to be accelerating at an alarming rate. You must be prepared to accept, even welcome change in your life. Instead of fighting change, make change work for you.

As your wheel roles down the road of life, you will be presented with choices, challenges and opportunities. Will you embrace those challenges with the optimism of a fully-functioning human being capable of conquering any obstacle placed in the way? Or will you avoid those challenges, play it safe and never know the ecstasy of supreme triumph?

Life is never easy. Sacrifices may be required to realize your dreams. Which sacrifices are you ready to accept in the pursuit of your dreams? Life is always a balancing act. Only you can make the decision to follow your dreams, change your life and live the quality life.

Sharing my Quality of Life experiences with you has been a fulfillment of one of my dreams. I hope I have touched your life in a positive way. I wish you well, my friend. It would be my privilege to meet you along the way and share experiences.

> **May the road rise to meet you.**
> **May the wind be always at your back.**
>
> **May the sunshine warm up your face.**
> **May the rain fall soft upon your bed.**
>
> **And until we meet again,**
> **May God hold you in the**
> **Hollow of his hand.**
>
> — **Irish Blessing**

Epilogue

I have been fortunate in knowing many people living quality lives. Two of these people have particularly influenced my life.

I met Jean Chevalier Peterson in 1954 while I was serving as a warrant officer in the California Army National Guard. Jean, along with Bryce J. Brisbin, went out of his way to help me obtain commissioned officer status. He has remained my mentor and friend for the past 40 years.

Jean adored his wife, Grayce, who suffered from poor health after injuries incurred during a violent storm at sea. As Grayce's health deteriorated, Jean cared for her until the end of her life with the devotion only found between people deeply in love with each other.

Jean now lives in Sedona, Arizona, where he is an active member of the community. He served on the county planning commission, as a volunteer with the Sedona Visitors Center and as a docent at the Northern Arizona Museum. Jean has become involved in learning the history, customs and culture of Native Americans.

While Jean displays a tough guy image, underneath, he is a *teddy bear* with real feelings. I have been deeply touched by the love this man has given to me during our 40 year friendship.

Like Jean, Abel Medeiros has seldom met a stranger who does not shortly become a friend. My wife, Roberta, and I first met Abel when he introduced himself to us at a Portuguese Cultural Festival. Abel welcomed us and made us feel accepted in his community.

Abel Medeiros demonstrated the *Aloha* spirit found among so many Hawaiians. In Hawaii, *ohana* means family, and Abel proceeded to include us as part of his extended family. We came to learn that Abel is well known as a man who regularly reaches out to others and brings them into his wide and ever expanding circle of friends.

Throughout his 70 plus years, Abel has played an active role in life on the Hawaiian island of Kauai. He has served as a State Senator and on the County Council. In addition, he is a committed Christian, active in supporting and serving his church.

His wonderful sense of humor balanced by his grounded, practical, level-headed realism and his genuine love for people exemplify a person whose life is worthy of emulation by others. His sphere of influence and generosity of spirit touches so many in his family and community, that those of us who are fortunate enough to know him feel truly blessed.

To me, Jean and Abel are living examples of people who have experienced Quality of Life in totality, encompassing all eight factors in ever widening circles of enriching life experiences.

My respect and love for Jean Chevalier Peterson and Abel Medeiros is beyond measure. I hope there are people in your life as fine as these two men.

About the Author

H. Stanley Jones walks his talk and knows first hand about that of which he writes and speaks. He is a husband, father, grandfather, entrepreneur, and lifetime student who was born and raised in Decatur, Illinois. He served 35 years in the Army Reserves, Illinois and California National Guard, and on active duty, rising in rank from Private to Lieutenant Colonel. Stan served as the elected City Treasurer of Inglewood, California for nearly 25 years.

Stan earned three degrees in three separate fields from Northrop University, University of Southern California, and UCLA and has earned the designations of a Certified Speaking Professional, Certified Association Executive and Certified Public Accountant. Each was acquired in the minimum possible time and he is the only person to hold all three.

Quality of Life: About the Author

Dr. H. Stanley Jones is a professional speaker, seminar leader and entrepreneur who has taught full time on four campuses of the California State University system as well as being a faculty member at other universities.

In addition to this book, he is the author of *Planning Your Financial Future: Personal Financial Planning that Helps You* and *Marketing Your Financial Planning Services: A Guide for Professionals*. Stan is also the founder of the Quality of Life Institute.

I would very much like to hear from any of you wishing to share stories of how my book helped you find balance and quality in your life. Please write to me at:

> Dr. H. Stanley Jones
> Quality of Life Institute
> P.O. Box 951
> Kilauea, HI 96754

If you're interested in learning more about Quality of Life, I will be conducting seminars throughout the United States and Australia. Please call 800/227-3377 for more information.

Additional copies of my book *Quality of Life: Achieving Balance in an Unbalanced World* are available by writing to me at the above address or calling 800/227-3377. Quality of Life audio cassette tapes are also available.

You may also order any of my other books. Please call for information. I look forward to hearing from each and every one of you.

Index

A

Abundant Living 158
Abuse 32
Accounting Today 69
Active 20-30 International 52
Addiction
   Alcohol 32, 54, 121, 161
   Drugs 32, 116, 159
Ageless Body, Timeless Mind 131
AgeLink 161
AIDS 55, 159
Alcohol 121
Alcoholics Anonymous
   (AA) 53, 161
Alcoholism 32
AMA Guidelines 128
American Heart Association Journal 117
Anderson, Dale ix
Angelou, Maya 44, 54
Apprenticeships 66
Ash, Stephen ix
Assets 92–93

Atherosclerosis 117
Automobile maintenance 122

B

Bach, Richard 35
Bacon, Francis (Sir) 14
Bakersfield Californian, The x, 51
Bakersfield College 160
Bargains 100–101
Bartolone, Vince 144
Batten, Joe ix
Bay of Pigs 84
Be (Happy) Attitudes, The 156
Beasley, Virgil 17
Beecher, Henry Ward 158
Benham, Herb x
Bentley, Rick x
Bergeson, Marian (Sen) ix
Bible, The 156
Big ticket purchases 98–99
Bigotry 46
Blood vessel disease 117

Bok, Derek 63
Brindamour, Jean-Louis ix
Brisbin, Bryce J. 171
Brothers, Sharon x, 160
Brown, Jerry 43
Burke, Edmund 50
Burns, George 133
Burrus, Daniel 17
Burton, Charles 144
Buscaglia, Leo 12

C

California
   Conservation Corps 44
   Medfly infestation 43
Cancer 116
Canfield, Jack ix
Career 20, 73–90
   Aptitude 76, 89
   Attitude 76, 80
   Change 82, 84–85
   Compensation 89
   Counselors 76
   Motivation 81
   Objectives 77
   Perspective 78–79
Carroll, Lewis 93
Cathcart, Jim 16
Checkers 149
Checkups 128
Chinese Proverb 93
Chopra, Deepak 131
Churchill, Winston 29
Circulation 117
Civil disobedience 158
Cliques 45
Collins, B.T. 43–44

Commitment to excellence 90
Community 19, 39–56
   Building 55
   Definition 39
   Differences as gifts 45
   Global 56
   Sharing 54
   Spirit 54
Compassion 164
Compounding 104
CompuServe 68
Computers 68, 102, 138–139
   Bulletin boards 40, 68
Confidence 164
Confucius 153
Consumption 100
Correspondence courses 65
Cowley, Abraham 165
Cox, Danny 81
Crawford, Jean ix
Crisp, Michael ix
Crystal Cathedral, The 154, 156
Cuban missile crisis 84

D

Dalai Lama 152
Damien, Father 159
Delegate 146
Denny, Reginald 163
Dewey, John 57
Diabetes 116
*Different Drum: Community Making
   and Peace, The* x, 55
Diller, Phyllis 122
   Fang (her husband) 122
Discovery Channel, The 69
Disney 165

Quality of Life: Index

Dodgers, Los Angeles 139
Donahue, Phil 41
Donne, John 47
Donnelly, Susan 16
Dotson, Rika vii
Dreams 10–11
  Goals vs. 10–12
Driving 122–124
Dubin, Burt 17
Durant, Will and Ariel 26
Dysfunctional families 31

E

Eagles, Gil 118
Eastman, George 150
Education 19–20, 57–72
  Audio tapes 67
  Children 60
  Co-operative 66
  Concept of 58
  Continuing 66–67
  Cost of 63
  Crime and 63
  Dropouts 64
  Employment opportunities and 62–63
  Extended studies 66–67
  Liberal 62
  Video instruction 67
Eiseman, Leatrice viii
Enablers 32
Environment 87, 121
Epicetus 132
Erikson, E. 154
Ethical concepts 151
Exercise 150
Expenses 95–97

F

Family 18, 25–38
  Definition 25
  Intimacy 30
Fantasy Island *8*
Faranda, Thomas W. 16
Father Knows Best *25*
Feather, William 72
Fighting AIDS Through Education 159
Finances 21, 91–110, 110–114
Financial
  Delegate duties 95
  Goals 94, 106
  Habits
    Saving 97–101
  Health 92
  Liquidity 108
  Position 92
Florida Department of Education 63
Flynn, Clarence E. 77
Forgiveness 34, 162-163
Fowler, E. 154
Fox, Arnold ix, 117, 119
Frank, Mike ix, 15
Franklin, Benjamin 103, 118
Friendship 91
Fripp, Patricia 80
Further Along the Road Less Traveled x, 154–155

G

Gamblers Anonymous 161
George, David Lloyd 23
Ghandi, Mahatma 158
Gifts Differing 44

Goals   145
God   151–152, 152, 156, 158, 165
Golden Rule, The   152
Grandy, Jeff   84–85
Grass, Günter   49
Gulf War   55

H

Hackett, Buddy   163
Hansen, Mark Victor   17
Hawaii, Molokai   159
Health   21–22, 115–134
   Emotional   130–132
      Support Groups   130
      Therapy   130
   Genes and   116
   Mental. *See* stress
Heart attack   117
Heart disease   116, 117
Heckler, Lou   17, 28
Henry, Robert   ix
Hernandez, Francis   x, 159
High blood pressure   128
High cholesterol   128
Higher power   161
Hill, Napoleon   83
Hiroshima!   84
Hirsh, Sandra Krebs   76
HIV   159
Hobby   140
Holmes, Oliver W.   58
Homeowner's association   50
Hoover, W.H.   80
Hughes, Bert   ix, 107, 112
Humility   164

I

I Am A Rock   50
Ibsen, Henrik   53
Illness
   Symptoms   128
Immune For Life   119
Income   101–103, 109
India   157
Inflation   112
Insurance   89
Interactive communication   69–70
Interest   104
Interest rates   104, 106, 109
Internal Revenue Service   109
Investing   103
Investment goals   106
Investment Pyramid   112
Investments   100, 110, 113
   Home   108–109
      Purchase costs   110
      Remodeling   110
      Selling costs   110
   Risks   110–112
      Diversification   112
Iranian Hostages   55
Irish Blessing   165
Is the Kingdom of God Realism   158

J

Jackson, Jesse   28
James, William   13
Jefferson, Thomas   119
Jeffries, Elizabeth   16
Jiminy Cricket   165
Johnson, Lyndon   60
Johnson, Samuel   103

Quality of Life: Index

Jones, E. Stanley 157
Jones, Hal 64–65
Jones, Roberta vii
Judaism 156
Jung, Carl 11
Junior League 52

K

Keeler, Connie x
Keller, Helen 12
Kelly, John B. ix, 96, 114
Kennedy, John F. 62, 72
King, Dr. Martin Luther, Jr. 158
King, Larry 41
King, Rodney 163
Klein, Ruth L. 15
Kohlberg 154

L

Leadership 52–53
Learning Channel, The 69
Lease
  Purchase vs. 100
Leisure 22, 135–150
  definition 135
Lemmon, Jack 73
Lepers 159
Lewis, Randy 63
Liabilities 93
Libraries 68
Life Expectancy 116
Limbaugh, Rush 41
Linkletter, Art ix, 14, 116
Lombardi, Vince 90
Love 38

M

Mackay, Harvey 74
Madwed, Sidney 17
Magazines 69
Mahatma Ghandi 158
Management 85–86
Mandino, Og ix
Manning, Marilyn 16
Marriage 29–31
Marshall, Sol viii
Masquelier, Roger 59
Mathews, James K.
  (Bishop) ix, 157
Maurois, Andre 26
MBTI. *See* Myers Briggs
  Temperament Indicator
McDargh, Eileen 16
McFarland, Kenneth 12
McLuhan, Marshall 136
McMurray, Barbara 51
Medical history, personal 116
Medeiros, Abel 172
Memory jogger 70–71
Methodist 157
Michelangelo 59
Microfilm 68
Mihalap, Hope 46
Mills, Sharon viii, 35
Milton 14
Mitchell, W. 82
Money
  Time Value of 100, 105
Monopoly 149
Mother Teresa 159
Morse, Dr. Harold E. 69
Mothers Against Drunk Driving
  (M.A.D.D.) 163
Movies 141

Myers, Isabell Briggs 44, 76
Myers, Peter B. 44
Myers-Briggs Type Indicator 76–77

N

National Commission on Sleep Disorders Research 125
National Institute of Business Management 81
National Speakers Association ix
Neighborhood Watch x, 51
Net Worth 93, 95
Newman, James W. 16
Newspapers 69
Newton, Joseph F. 41
Nobel Peace Prize 157

O

Ohio, Canton 80
Opportunity
  Loss 100
Organ transplants 129
Overeaters Anonymous 161

P

P.O.W. bracelets 55
Pantone Color Institute viii
Parent Teacher Association 49
Paulson, Terry ix, 13, 47, 49
Peale, Norman Vincent 156
Pearsall, Paul x, 78
Peck, M. Scott x, 55, 154, 156
Perfectionism 147–148

Personal Power 164
Personality
  Type A 140
Peterson, Jean C. ix, 171–172
Photography 140
Piaget, J. 154
Pickard, William M., Jr.(Rev) ix
Platinum Rule, The 152
Play 138. *See also* Recreation
Politics 49
Pollution 121
Pope, Alexander 162
Potter, Paul 88
Power of Positive Thinking, The 156
Poynter, Dan ix
Prayer 151
Present value 105
Priorities
  "To Do" lists 147
Procrastination 148
PRODIGY Interactive Personal Service 40, 68
Prosper 50
Proverbs
  Arabian 115
  Chinese 59, 71
  Old 133
Psalm 111 156
Psychic income 86

Q

Quality of Life
  Seminars 148
Qubein, Nido ix, 15, 47–48

R

"Random Acts of Senseless Kindness" 160
Raphäel, Sally Jessy 41
Recreation 138. *See also* Play
Reputation, company 87
Retirement 106–108, 113. *See also* Savings
Retirement plans 89
Rhode, Naomi ix
Riots, Los Angeles 163
Risk management 113
Road Less Traveled, The 156
Robinson, John 144
Rockefeller, John D., Jr. 50
Roosevelt, Eleanor 9
Rumph, Myrtle Faye 162

S

Safety 122–125
Sales tax 99–100
Salsbury, Glenna ix
Sanborn, Mark ix, 136
Savings 103, 107–108
   Goals 108
Schuller, Robert 13, 154, 156
Scott, Willard 30
Sears Roebuck 88
Seat belt 123
Selbert, Roger 137
Self-esteem 160
SES. *See also* Socio-Economic Status
Shakespeare, William 132
Shaw, George Bernard 27, 92, 133
Silver Rule, The 153
Simon and Garfunkel 50

Sleep 125–127
   Alcohol and effect on 127
   Amount of 125
   Caffeine and effect on 127
   Deficit 125
   Deprivation 126
   Disorders 125
   Habits 126
   Inducer 127
   Loss of. *See also* Sleep Deficit
   Naps and 128
   Patterns of 125, 126, 128
   Positions 126–127
   Sleeping pills 127
   Temperature 126
Smoke alarms 124
Smoking 121–122
   Second-hand smoke 122
Socio-Economic Status (SES) 117
Spangler, Murray 80
Spiering, Renee ix, 33
Spirituality 22–23, 151–166
   Definition 151
   Stages
      Chaotic/Antisocial 155
      Formal/Institutional 155
      Mystical/Communal 155
      Skeptical/Individual 155
   vs. religion 154
Sports 139
Stevens, Carl 161
Stress 120, 131–132, 150
Stress management 131–132
Stroke 117
Successful People *10*
Super Joy: In Love With Living x, 78
Supreme being 151
Swedenborg, Emanuel 165

T

Tansey, Dave ix
Taxes
  Benefits 110
  Withholdings 109
Television 69, 137
Ten Commandments 152
Teresa, Mother 159
"Three D's of Work" 79
Time management 144–146
  Organization 145
Trade schools 65
Travel 141–142
Trident submarine 85
Tryptophan 127
Twain, Mark 117
Twelve Step program 161
Twisted Tale, A ix, 33
Tz'u, Tauan-mu 153

U

UCLA. *See also* University of California, Los Angeles
University of California, Los Angeles 133
University of Maryland 144
Using the Myers-Briggs Type Indicator in Organizations x, 76

V

Vacation 141–142
Victorious Living 158
Vietnam 43, 55

W

Wall, Chuck x, 160
Walters, Dorothy (Dottie) 15, 59–60
Warner, Carolyn ix
Water 119
Weight control 117–120
  Behavior modification 118
  Calories 118
  Diet 118
  Exercise 119–121
    Walking 120
  Nutrition 118
  Super Food Diet 119
Welch, Tamara x
Whitman, Walt 166
Winfrey, Oprah 41
Worship 154
Wouldn't Take Nothing for My Journey Now 44

Z

Zoo News 69